DK

EYEWITNESS TRAVEL GUIDES

FRENCH
PHRASE BOOK

A Dorling Kindersley Book

LONDON, NEW YORK, MUNICH,
MELBOURNE, AND DELHI

Compiled by Lexus Ltd with Valérie Dupin and Karen McAulay
Published in the United States by DK Publishing
345 Hudson Street, New York, NY 10014

First American Edition 1998
Reprinted with corrections 2000, 2003
14 15 16 22 21 20
026-ED120-Mar/03

Dorling Kindersley books can be purchased in bulk quantities at discounted
prices for use in promotions or as premiums. We are also able to offer special
editions and personalized jackets, corporate imprints, and excerpts from all of
our books, tailored specifically to meet your own needs. To find out more,
please contact: Special Markets Department, Dorling Kindersley Publishing,
345 Hudson Street, New York, NY 10014; Fax 212-689-5254.

Library of Congress Cataloging-in-Publication Data.
French phrase book. -- 1st American ed.
        p,   cm, -- (Dorling Kindersly travel guides phrase books)
    First Published in Great Britain in 1997
by Dorling Kindersly Ltd.
    Includes index.
    ISBN 978-0-7894-9487-0 (alk.paper)
    1. French language--Conversation and phrasebooks--
English. I.DK Publishing   II. Series.
PC2121.F817   1998
448.3'421--dc21   97-47222
                                                             CIP

Printed and bound in China by Leo Paper Products Limited

see our complete catalogue at
www.dk.com

CONTENTS

PREFACE

This *Dorling Kindersley Eyewitness Travel Guides Phrase Book* has been compiled by experts to meet the general needs of tourists and business travelers. Arranged under headings such as Hotels, Driving, and so forth, the ample selection of useful words and phrases is supported by a 2,000-line mini-dictionary. There is also an extensive menu guide listing approximately 600 dishes or methods of cooking and presentation.

Typical replies to questions you may ask during your trip, and the signs or instructions you may see or hear, are shown in tinted boxes. In the main text, the pronunciation of French words and phrases is imitated in English sound syllables. The Introduction gives basic guidelines to French pronunciation.

Dorling Kindersley Eyewitness Travel Guides are recognized as the world's best travel guides. Each title features specially commissioned color photographs, detailed maps, cutaways of major buildings and 3-D aerial views, plus information on sights, events, hotels, restaurants, shopping, and entertainment.

Dorling Kindersley Eyewitness Travel Guides titles include:

France · Loire Valley · Paris · Provence · Amsterdam · Australia
Sydney · Berlin · Budapest · California · Florida · Hawaii
New York · San Francisco & Northern California · Canada
Great Britain · London · Ireland · Dublin · Scotland
Greece: Athens & the Mainland · The Greek Islands · Istanbul
Italy · Florence & Tuscany · Milan & the Lakes · Naples · Rome
Sardinia · Sicily · Venice & the Veneto · Jerusalem & the Holy Land
Mexico · Moscow · St. Petersburg · Portugal · Lisbon · Prague
South Africa · Spain · Barcelona · Madrid · Seville & Andalusia
Thailand · Vienna · Warsaw

INTRODUCTION

PRONUNCIATION

When reading the imitated pronunciation, the same value should be given to all syllables, since there is hardly any stress in French words. Pronounce each syllable as if it formed part of an English word and you will be understood. Remember the points below, and your pronunciation will be even closer to the correct French.

an   represents the nasal sound as in **vin**, **un**, and **main**
—similar to saying "an" without sounding the "n"
g   is pronounced hard as in "get"
i   pronounced as "eye"
j   like the "s" sound in "leisure"
on   represents the nasal sound as in **bon**, **en**, and **temps**
—similar to saying "on" without sounding the "n"
oo   is how we imitate the French "u" (say "seen" with your lips rounded as if you were about to whistle, and the result will be close enough)

USE OF THE FRENCH WORD "ON"

Phrases involving "I" or "we" and impersonal phrases have sometimes been translated with the French word "on." For example: **Can I camp here?** Est-ce qu'on peut camper ici? Literally, "on" means "one," but is not a formal word like it is in English.

GENDERS AND ARTICLES

French has two genders for nouns—masculine and feminine. We generally give the definite article ("the")—**le** for masculine nouns, **la** for feminine nouns, and **les** for plural nouns. Where the indefinite article ("a, an") is more appropriate, we have used **un** for masculine and **une** for feminine nouns or the words for "some," **du** (masculine), **de la** (feminine), and **des** (plural).

USEFUL EVERYDAY PHRASES

Yes, No, OK, etc.

Yes/no
Oui/non
wee/non

Excellent!
Parfait!
parfeh

Don't!
Non!
non

OK
D'accord
dakkor

That's fine
C'est bien
seh byan

That's right
C'est exact
set exakt

Greetings, Introductions

How do you do, pleased to meet you
Enchanté (de faire votre connaissance)
onshontay duh fair vottr konnessonss

Good morning
Bonjour
bonjoor

Good evening/Good night
Bonsoir
b<u>on</u>swahr

Goodbye
Au revoir
oh-rvwahr

How are you?
Comment allez-vous?
komm<u>ont</u> allay voo

(familiar form)
Comment ça va?
komm<u>on</u> sa va

My name is …
Je m'appelle …
juh mappell

What's your name?
Comment vous appelez-vous?
komm<u>on</u> vooz appellay voo

(familiar form)
Comment tu t'appelles?
komm<u>on</u> t<u>oo</u> tappell

What's his/her name?
Comment s'appelle-t-il/s'appelle-t-elle?
komm<u>on</u> sappellteel/sappelltell

May I introduce …?
Puis-je vous présenter …?
pwee<u>j</u> voo pray<u>zon</u>tay

This is …
Voici …
vwah-see

Hello/Hi!
Bonjour/Salut!
b<u>on</u>joor/sal<u>oo</u>

Bye!
Salut!
sal<u>oo</u>

See you soon
A bientôt
ah byantoh

It's been nice meeting you *(said by a man/woman)*
J'ai été heureux/heureuse de faire votre connaissance
jay aytay uhruh/uhruhz duh fair vottr konnessonss

PLEASE, THANK YOU, APOLOGIES

Thank you/No, thank you
Merci/Non, merci
mairsee/non mairsee

Please
S'il vous plaît
seel voo pleh

Excuse me!/Sorry!
Pardon!
pardon

I'm really sorry
Je suis vraiment désolé
juh swee vraymon dayzolay

It was my fault/it wasn't my fault
C'était de ma faute/ce n'était pas de ma faute
sayteh duh ma foht/suh nayteh pa duh ma foht

WHERE, HOW, ASKING

Excuse me, please
Pardon
pardon

Can you tell me …?
Pouvez-vous me dire …?
poovay voo muh deer

May I have …?
Est-ce que je pourrais avoir …?
esskuh juh poorray avwah

Would you like a …?
Est-ce que vous voulez un/une …?
esskuh voo voolay <u>an</u>/<u>oo</u>n

Would you like to …?
Est-ce que vous voulez …?
esskuh voo voolay

Is there … here?
Est-ce qu'il y a … ici?
esskeel-ya … ee-see

What's that?
Qu'est-ce que c'est?
kesskuh seh

How much is it?
Combien ça coûte?
k<u>on</u>by<u>an</u> sa koot

Where is the …?
Où est le/la …?
oo eh luh/la

Is there wheelchair access?
Y a-t-il un accès pour les personnes à mobilité réduite?
eeahteel onaksay poor lay payrson ah mobeelitay raydooeet

Are there facilities for the disabled?
Y a-t-il des aménagements pour recevoir des personnes à
  mobilité réduite?
*eeahteel day zamaynajuhmon poor ruhsuhvwahr day payrson ah
  mobeelitay raydooeet*

Are guide dogs allowed?
Les chiens guide sont-ils admis?
lay sheean geed sontel admee?

ABOUT ONESELF

I'm from …
Je viens de …
juh vyan duh

I'm … years old
J'ai … ans
jay … on

I'm a …
Je suis …
juh swee

I'm married/single/divorced
Je suis marié/célibataire/divorcé
juh swee maree-ay/sayleebatair/deevorssay

I have … sisters/brothers/children
J'ai … soeurs/frères/enfants
jay … suhr/frair/onfon

LIKES, DISLIKES, SOCIALIZING

I like/love …
J'aime/j'adore …
jem/jador

I don't like …
Je n'aime pas …
juh nem pa

I hate …
Je déteste …
juh daytest

Do you like …?
Aimez-vous …?
aymay voo

It's delicious/awful!
C'est délicieux/horrible!
seh dayleess-yuh/orreeb-l

I don't drink/smoke
Je ne bois pas/ne fume pas
juh nuh bwah pa/nuh foom pa

Do you mind if I smoke?
Cela ne vous ennuie pas que je fume?
suhla nuh vooz onwee pa kuh juh foom

I don't eat meat or fish
Je ne mange ni viande ni poisson
juh nuh monj nee vee-ond nee pwass-on

What would you like to drink?
Qu'est-ce que vous voulez boire?
kesskuh voo voolay bwahr

I would like a …
Je voudrais un/une …
juh voodreh an/oon

Nothing for me, thanks
Rien pour moi, merci
ryan poor mwah mairsee

I'll get this one
C'est moi qui offre
seh mwah kee offr

Cheers! *(toast)*
Santé!
sontay

I would like to …
J'aimerais …
jemmereh

Let's go to Versailles/the movies
Allons à Versailles/au cinéma
allonz ah vairsi/oh seenayma

Let's go swimming/for a walk
Allons nager/nous balader
allon najay/noo baladay

What's the weather like?
Quel temps fait-il?
kell ton feteel

The weather's awful
Le temps est affreux
luh ton et affruh

It's pouring down
Il pleut à verse
eel pluh a vairs

It's really hot/it's very sunny
Il fait vraiment chaud/il fait beaucoup de soleil
eel feh vrehmon shoh/eel feh bohkoo duh solay

HELP, PROBLEMS (SEE ALSO EMERGENCIES p108)

Can you help me?
Pouvez-vous m'aider?
poovay voo mayday

I don't understand
Je ne comprends pas
juh nuh konpron pa

Do you speak English/German/Spanish?
Est-ce que vous parlez anglais/allemand/espagnol?
esskuh voo parlay ongleh/allmon/espan-yol

Does anyone here speak English?
Est-ce qu'il y a quelqu'un ici qui parle anglais?
esskeel-ya kellkan ee-see kee parl ongleh

I can't speak French
Je ne parle pas français
juh nuh parl pa fronseh

I don't know
Je ne sais pas
juh nuh seh pa

What's wrong?
Qu'est-ce qui ne va pas?
kesskee nuh va pa

Please speak more slowly
Pouvez-vous parler plus lentement, s'il vous plaît?
poovay voo parlay ploo lontmon seel voo pleh

Please write it down for me
Pouvez-vous me l'écrire, s'il vous plaît?
poovay voo muh laykreer seel voo pleh

I've lost my way
Je me suis perdu
juh me swee pairdoo

Go away!
Allez-vous-en!
allay vooz on

TALKING TO RECEPTIONISTS, ETC.

I have an appointment with …
J'ai rendez-vous avec …
jay rondayvoo avek

I'd like to see …
J'aimerais voir …
jemmereh vwahr

Here's my card
Voici ma carte
vwah-see ma kart

My company is …
Ma compagnie est …
ma konpan-yee eh

May I use your phone?
Est-ce que je peux utiliser votre téléphone?
esskuh juh puh ooteeleezay vottr taylayfon

THINGS YOU'LL HEAR

à bientôt	see you later
attention!	look out!
au revoir	goodbye
bien	fine
bon!	right! OK!
bonjour	hello
bon voyage!	have a good trip!
c'est correct	that's right
comment allez-vous?	how are you?
comment ça va?	how are things?
de rien	you're welcome
enchanté	pleased to meet you
entrez	come in
excusez-moi	excuse me
je ne comprends pas	I don't understand
je ne sais pas	I don't know
je suis vraiment désolé!	I'm so sorry!
je vous en prie	don't mention it
merci	thank you
merci beaucoup	thank you very much
merci, pareillement	thank you, the same to you
non	no
oui	yes
papiers, s'il vous plaît	identification papers, please
pardon!/pardon?	sorry!/pardon?

→

précisément	exactly
qu'est-ce que vous avez dit?	what did you say?
ravi de faire votre connaissance	how do you do, nice to meet you
salut!	hi!
servez-vous	help yourself
si	yes
très bien, merci —et vous?	very well, thank you —and you?
voici	here you are
vraiment?	is that right?

THINGS YOU'LL SEE

accueil	reception
ascenseur	elevator
à vendre	for sale
caisse	cash register, cashier
complet	full, no vacancies
dames	women
défense de …	forbidden
eau non potable	not drinking water
eau potable	drinking water
emplacement réservé	reserved parking
en dérangement/en panne	out of order
entrée	entrance
entrée gratuite	free admission
entrée libre	free admission
entrez sans frapper	enter without knocking
fermé	closed
fermeture annuelle	annual closure
fermeture automatique des portes	doors close automatically
frappez avant d'entrer	knock before entering

→

15

fumeurs	smoking
heures de visite	visiting hours
heures d'ouverture	opening times
il est interdit de marcher sur les pelouses	keep off the grass
interdiction de fumer	no smoking
interdit(e)	forbidden, prohibited
jour férié	national holiday
libre	free, vacant
messieurs	men
ne pas ... sous peine d'amende	do not ... on penalty of fine
non-fumeurs	no smoking
occupé	occupied
ouvert	open
passage interdit	no entry
payez ici	pay here
peinture fraîche	wet paint
poussez	push
premier étage	first floor
prière de ...	please ...
privé	private
renseignements	inquiries
réservé	reserved
rez-de-chaussée	ground floor
route	road
rue	street
rue piétonne/rue piétonnière	shopping center
sans issue	dead end
sortie	exit
sortie de secours	emergency exit
sous-sol	basement
syndicat d'initiative	tourist information
tirez	pull
veuillez ...	please ...

COLLOQUIALISMS

You may hear these. To use some of them yourself could be risky!

arnaque	rip-off, swindle
bagnole	car
barbant	boring
bécane	bike
bon sang de merde!	hell!
borne	kilometer
bouffe	food
bourré	drunk
ça alors!	I don't believe it!
c'est pas mon truc	it's not my sort of thing
chiche!	you're on!
cinglé	nut, nutcase
copain	pal, friend
crado	filthy
tu débloques!	you're crazy!
dingue	crazy
fringues	gear
génial!	great! fantastic!
machin	thing, thingamajig
mec	guy
merde!	shit!
mioche	kid, brat
nana	girl
paumé	done for, had it
pote	pal, friend
prendre un pot	to have a drink
salaud	S.O.B
super!	great!
sympa	nice
truc	thing, thingamajig
vachement ...	damn(ed) ...

DAYS, MONTHS, SEASONS

Sunday	dimanche	*deemonsh*
Monday	lundi	*landee*
Tuesday	mardi	*mardee*
Wednesday	mercredi	*mairkruhdee*
Thursday	jeudi	*juhdee*
Friday	vendredi	*vondruhdee*
Saturday	samedi	*sammdee*
January	janvier	*jonvee-ay*
February	février	*fayvree-ay*
March	mars	*marss*
April	avril	*ahvreel*
May	mai	*meh*
June	juin	*jwan*
July	juillet	*jwee-ay*
August	août	*oo*
September	septembre	*septonbr*
October	octobre	*oktobr*
November	novembre	*novonbr*
December	décembre	*dayssonbr*
Spring	le printemps	*pranton*
Summer	l'été	*laytay*
Fall	l'automne	*lohton*
Winter	l'hiver	*leevair*
Christmas	Noël	*noh-el*
Christmas Eve	la veille de Noël	*vay duh noh-el*
Good Friday	Vendredi saint	*vondredee san*
Easter	Pâques	*pak*
New Year	le Nouvel An	*noovel on*
New Year's Eve	la veille du Jour de l'an	*vay doo joor duh lon*
Pentecost	la Pentecôte	*pontkoht*

NUMBERS

0 zéro *zayro*
1 un, une *an, oon*
2 deux *duh*
3 trois *trwah*
4 quatre *kattr*
5 cinq *sank*
6 six *seess*
7 sept *set*
8 huit *weet*
9 neuf *nuhf*

10 dix *deess*
11 onze *onz*
12 douze *dooz*
13 treize *trez*
14 quatorze *kattorz*
15 quinze *kanz*
16 seize *sez*
17 dix-sept *deess-set*
18 dix-huit *deess-weet*
19 dix-neuf *deess-nuhf*

20 vingt *van*
21 vingt et un *vantay an*
22 vingt-deux *van duh*
30 trente *tront*
40 quarante *karront*
50 cinquante *sankont*
60 soixante *swassont*
70 soixante-dix *swassont-deess*
80 quatre-vingts *kattruhvan*
90 quatre-vingt-dix *kattruh-vandeess*
100 cent *son*
110 cent-dix *sondeess*
200 deux cents *duh-son*
1,000 mille *meel*
10,000 dix mille *deess meel*
20,000 vingt mille *van meel*
100,000 cent mille *son meel*
1,000,000 un million *meel-ion*

TIME

today	aujourd'hui	*ohjoord-wee*
yesterday	hier	*yair*
tomorrow	demain	*duhman*
the day before yesterday	avant-hier	*avont-yair*
the day after tomorrow	après-demain	*apreh-duhman*
this week	cette semaine	*set suhmen*
last week	la semaine dernière	*suhmen dairnee-air*
next week	la semaine prochaine	*suhmen proshen*
this morning	ce matin	*suh mattan*
this afternoon	cet après-midi	*set apreh-meedee*
this evening/ tonight	ce soir	*suh swahr*
yesterday afternoon	hier après-midi	*yair apreh-meedee*
last night	hier soir	*yair swahr*
tomorrow morning	demain matin	*duhman mattan*
tomorrow night	demain soir	*duhman swahr*
in three days	dans trois jours	*don trwah joor*
three days ago	il y a trois jours	*eelya trwah joor*
late	tard	*tar*
early	tôt	*toh*
soon	bientôt	*byantoh*
later on	plus tard	*ploo tar*
at the moment	pour le moment, maintenant	*poor luh momon, mantnon*
second	une seconde	*suhgond*
minute	une minute	*meenoot*
ten minutes	dix minutes	*dee meenoot*
quarter of an hour	un quart d'heure	*kar dur*
half an hour	une demi-heure	*duhmee ur*
three quarters of an hour	trois quarts d'heure	*trwah kar dur*

hour	une heure	*ur*
day	un jour	*joor*
every day	chaque jour	*shak joor*
all day	toute la journée	*toot la joornay*
the next day	le lendemain	*luh <u>lo</u>ndluhm<u>a</u>n*
week	une semaine	*suhmen*
two weeks	quinze jours,	*<u>kanz</u> joor,*
	deux semaines	*duh suhmen*
month	un mois	*mwah*
year	une année, un an	*annay, <u>on</u>*

TELLING TIME

The 24-hour clock is always used in the written form in timetables and for appointments, and also verbally in inquiry offices and if talking about the times of television and radio programs. However, in most other situations, people will use the 12-hour clock.

"What time is it?" is **quelle heure est-il?**. "O'clock" is translated as **heure(s)**, meaning "hour(s)." "(It's) one o'clock" is **(il est) une heure**; "(it's) four o'clock" is **(il est) quatre heures** and so on.

To denote the half hour use **et demie**, so "5:30" is **cinq heures et demie**.

To express minutes after the hour, state the hour followed by the number of minutes. For example, "ten past five" is **cinq heures dix**. For minutes to the hour use **moins**, which means "less." For example, "twenty to eleven" is **onze heures moins vingt**.

"Quarter" is **quart**, so "quarter past three" is **trois heures et quart**, and "quarter to eight" is **huit heures moins le quart**. The word "at" in phrases such as "at quarter past two" can be translated as **à**: **à deux heures et quart**.

The expressions "AM" and "PM" have no exact equivalents but the words **du matin** "in the morning," **de l'après-midi** "in the afternoon," and **du soir** "in the evening" or "at night" are used to distinguish between times that might otherwise be confused. For example, "5 AM" is **cinq heures du matin** and "5 PM" is **cinq heures de l'après-midi**; "11 AM" is **onze heures du matin** and "11 PM" is **onze heures du soir**.

AM	du matin	*doo matan*
PM (*afternoon*)	de l'après-midi	*duh lapreh-meedee*
(*evening*)	du soir	*doo swahr*
one o'clock	une heure	*oon ur*
ten past one	une heure dix	*oon ur deess*
quarter past one	une heure et quart	*oon ur ay kar*
twenty past two	deux heures vingt	*duhz ur van*
1:30	une heure et demie	*oon ur ay duhmee*
twenty to two	deux heures moins vingt	*duhz ur mwan van*
quarter to two	deux heures moins le quart	*duhz ur mwan luh kar*
two o'clock	deux heures	*duhz ur*
13:00 (1 PM)	treize heures	*trez ur*
16:30 (4:30 PM)	seize heures trente	*sez ur tront*
at seven o'clock	à sept heures	*ah set ur*
noon	midi	*meedee*
midnight	minuit	*meenwee*

THE CALENDAR

The cardinal numbers on page 19 are used to express the date in French with the exception of "the first," when the ordinal number is used:

June first	le premier juin	*luh pruhm-yay jwan*
August second	le deux août	*luh duh oo*
May twentieth	le vingt mai	*luh van meh*
May twenty-first	le vingt-et-un mai	*luh vant ay an meh*

HOTELS

France has over 17,000 hotels officially classified as Tourist Hotels by the Ministère du Commerce. These are identified by a blue and white hexagonal-shaped sign that shows the exact category of the hotel. These categories are: one star HRT: plain but fairly comfortable hotel; two stars HT: good, average hotel; three stars HGTGC: very comfortable; four stars HTGC: top class hotel; L: luxury hotel.

In addition to the officially classified Tourist Hotels, there are many others in which the rates, services, and amenities differ considerably. Among these are:

Relais de Tourisme: hotel with a limited number of rooms but offering food of a very good standard.
Relais Routiers: hotels, but mainly restaurants, situated on main roads. The food is excellent, the accommodations very reasonable, and the prices surprisingly low.
Relais Châteaux: usually of a very high standard and situated in beautiful and historical surroundings, they provide first-rate food.
Relais de Campagne: these are close to the main highways; most of them are in picturesque settings and all provide excellent food.
Logis et Auberges de France: this independent chain of mostly 1- and 2-star hotels situated off the beaten track gives the driver a rare opportunity to explore the deep countryside. They have to comply with a rigid set of standards in regard to food, service, and sanitation in order to get financial assistance from the State. The rates are very reasonable.

USEFUL WORDS AND PHRASES

balcony	un balcon	*balkon*
bathroom	la salle de bain	*sal duh ban*
bed	le lit	*lee*
bed and breakfast	chambre d'hôte	*shonbr doht*

bedroom	la chambre	*shonbr*
bill	la note	*not*
breakfast	le petit déjeuner	*puhtee day-juhnay*
dining room	la salle à manger	*sal ah monjay*
dinner	le dîner	*deenay*
double bed	un grand lit	*gran lee*
double room	une chambre pour	*shonbr poor duh*
	deux personnes	*pairson*
elevator	l'ascenseur	*assonssur*
foyer	le hall de réception	*ohl duh rayssep-sion*
full board	la pension complète	*ponss-ion konplet*
guesthouse	une pension de	*ponss-ion duh*
	famille	*famee*
half board	la demi-pension	*duhmee ponss-ion*
hotel	un hôtel	*oh-tell*
key	la clé, la clef	*klay*
lounge	le salon	*salon*
lunch	le déjeuner	*day-juhnay*
maid	la femme de chambre	*fam duh shonbr*
manager	le directeur	*deerektur*
parking lot	le parking	*par-keeng*
receipt	le reçu	*ruh-soo*
reception	la réception	*raysseps-ion*
receptionist	le/la réceptionniste	*raysseps-ioneest*
room	la chambre	*shonbr*
room service	le service en chambre	*sairveess on shonbr*
shower	la douche	*doosh*
single bed	un lit d'une personne	*lee doon pairson*
single room	une chambre pour	*shonbr poor oon*
	une personne	*pairson*
toilet	les toilettes	*twallet*
twin room	une chambre à deux lits	*shonbr ah duh lee*

Do you have any vacancies?
Avez-vous des chambres de libres?
avay voo day shonbr duh leebr

I have a reservation
J'ai réservé
jay rayzairvay

I'd like a single room
Je voudrais une chambre pour une personne
juh voodreh oon shonbr poor oon pairson

I'd like a room with a bathroom/balcony
Je voudrais une chambre avec salle de bain/balcon
juh voodreh oon shonbr avek sal duh ban/balkon

Is there satellite/cable TV in the rooms?
Les chambres ont-elles la télé par satellite/câblée?
Lay shoombr ontayl la taylay pahr satayleet/kablay

I'd like a room for one night/three nights
Je voudrais une chambre pour une nuit/trois nuits
juh voodreh oon shonbr poor oon nwee/trwah nwee

What is the charge per night?
Quel est le prix pour une nuit?
kell eh luh pree poor oon nwee

I don't know yet how long I'll stay
Je ne sais pas encore combien de temps je vais rester
juh nuh seh paz onkor konbyan duh ton juh veh restay

When is breakfast/dinner?
A quelle heure servez-vous le petit déjeuner/le dîner?
ah kell ur sairvay voo luh puhtee day-juhnay/luh deenay

Please wake/call me at … o'clock
Réveillez-moi à … heures, s'il vous plaît
rayvay-yay mwah ah … ur seel voo pleh

Can I have breakfast in my room?
Pouvez-vous me servir le petit déjeuner dans la chambre?
poovay voo meh sairveer luh puhtee day-juhnay don la shonbr

I'll be back at … o'clock
Je serai de retour à … heures
juh suhray duh ruhtoor ah … ur

My room number is …
Le numéro de ma chambre est …
luh noomayroh duh ma shonbr eh …

I'd like to have some laundry done
J'aimerais faire laver du linge
jemmereh fair lah-vay doo lanj

My reservation was for a double room
J'ai réservé une chambre pour deux personnes
jay rayzairvay oon shonbr poor duh pairson

I asked for a room with a private bathroom
J'ai demandé une chambre avec salle de bain attenante
jay duhmonday oon shonbr avek sal duh ban attuhnont

I need a light bulb
Il me faut une ampoule
eel muh foh oon onpool

There is no toilet paper in the bathroom
Il n'y a pas de papier toilettte dans la salle de bain
eel nya pa duh papee-ay twalet don la sal duh ban

The window won't open
Pas moyen d'ouvrir la fenêtre
pa mwi-an doovreer la fuhn-ettr

There isn't any hot water
Il n'y a pas d'eau chaude
eel nya pa doh shohd

The outlet in the bathroom doesn't work
La prise dans la salle de bain ne marche pas
la preez don la sal duh ban nuh marsh pa

I'm leaving tomorrow
Je pars demain
juh par duhman

When do I have to vacate the room?
A quelle heure dois-je libérer la chambre?
ah kell ur dwah juh leebayray la shonbr

Can I have the bill, please?
Pouvez-vous préparer ma note, s'il vous plaît?
poovay voo prayparay ma not seel voo pleh

I'll pay by credit card
Je payerai avec une carte de crédit
juh pay-uhray avek oon kart duh kraydee

I'll pay cash
Je payerai comptant
juh pay-uhray konton

Can you get me a taxi?
Pouvez-vous m'appeler un taxi?
poovay voo mapplay an taxee

Can you recommend another hotel?
Pouvez-vous recommander un autre hôtel?
poovay voo ruhkommonday an oht-r oh-tell

THINGS YOU'LL SEE

addition	bill
ascenseur	elevator
chambre d'hôte	bed and breakfast
complet	no vacancies
déjeuner	lunch
demi-pension	half board
douche	shower
entrée	entrance

→

27

entrée interdite	no admission
escalier	stairs
maison d'hôtes	guesthouse
pension	guesthouse
pension complète	full board
pension de famille	guesthouse
petit déjeuner	breakfast
poussez	push
privé	private
réservé	reserved
réservé au personnel	staff only
réservé aux clients de l'hôtel	hotel patrons only
salle de bain	bathroom
sortie de secours	emergency exit
tirez	pull

THINGS YOU'LL HEAR

Je suis désolé, mais nous sommes complets
I'm sorry, we're full

Nous n'avons plus de chambres pour deux personnes/une personne
There are no double/single rooms left

Pour combien de nuits?
For how many nights?

Comment payez-vous?
How will you be paying?

Veuillez payer d'avance
Please pay in advance

La chambre doit être libérée à midi
You must vacate the room by noon

CAMPING AND TRAILER TRAVEL

Campsites: there are more than 6,000 recognized campsites in France, graded from 1- to 4-stars. Most of these have an enclosure under constant supervision, running water, washing facilities, shower houses, bathrooms, a garbage collection service, and facilities for buying food in or near the camp.

Youth hostels: there are more than 300 youth hostels in France that are open to anybody who holds a YHA membership card. This card is valid all over the world. Most French hostels provide the bare essentials. For further information you should consult your own Youth Hostel Association or the Fédération Unie des Auberges de la Jeunesse.

USEFUL WORDS AND PHRASES

backpack	un sac à dos	*sak ah doh*
bucket	un seau	*soh*
camper *(RV)*	une caravane	*karavan*
camper site	un terrain de camping/caravaning	*terran duh konpeeng/ karavaneeng*
campfire	un feu de camp	*fuh duh kon*
go camping	faire du camping	*fair doo konpeeng*
campsite	un terrain de camping	*terran duh konpeeng*
cooking utensils	des ustensiles de cuisine	*oostonseel duh kweezeen*
drinking water	de l'eau potable	*oh pot-abl*
groundcloth	un tapis de sol	*tapee duh sol*
hitchhike	faire de l'autostop	*fair duh loh-tohstop*
rope	une corde	*kord*
saucepans	des casseroles	*kassrol*
sleeping bag	un sac de couchage	*sak duh kooshaj*
tent	une tente	*tont*
trash	les ordures	*ordoor*
youth hostel	une auberge de jeunesse	*oh-bairj duh juhness*

Can I camp here?
Est-ce qu'on peut camper ici?
esskon puh konpay ee-see

Can we park the camper (RV) here?
Est-ce qu'on peut garer la caravane ici?
esskon puh garray la karavan ee-see

Where is the nearest campsite/camper site?
Où se trouve le terrain de camping/caravaning le plus proche?
oo suh troov luh terran duh konpeeng/karavaneeng luh ploo prosh

What is the charge per night?
Quel est le prix pour une nuit?
kell eh luh pree poor oon nwee

How much is it for a week?
Ça coûte combien pour une semaine?
sa koot konbyan poor oon suhmen

I only want to stay for one night
Je veux rester une nuit seulement
juh vuh restay oon nwee suhlmon

We're leaving tomorrow
Nous partons demain
noo parton duhman

Where is the kitchen?
Où est la cuisine?
oo eh la kweezeen

Can I light a fire here?
Est-ce que je peux allumer un feu ici?
esskuh juh puh alloomay an fuh ee-see

Do you know where I can get ...?
Est-ce que vous savez où je peux trouver ...?
esskuh voo savay oo juh puh troovay

Is there drinking water here?
Est-ce qu'il y a de l'eau potable ici?
esskeel-ya duh loh pot-abl ee-see

THINGS YOU'LL SEE

allumer	to light
à louer	for rent
auberge de jeunesse	youth hostel
camping interdit	no camping
couverture	blanket
cuisine	kitchen
douches	showers
eau non potable	not drinking water
eau potable	drinking water
emplacement	site
entrée	entrance
feu	fire
gérant	manager
lavoir	washing facilities
lumière	light
recharge	refill
réchaud à gaz	gas stove
remorque	trailer
sac de couchage	sleeping bag
sanitaires	toilets and showers
tente	tent
terrain de camping	campsite
toile de tente	tent

VILLAS AND APARTMENTS

Rental accommodations are widely available. These can be a villa, a small cottage, an apartment, or part of a farmhouse.

You may be asked to pay for certain "extras" not included in the original price. You might want to ask if electricity, gas, etc., are included. It's a good idea to ask about an inventory of household goods at the start, rather than be told something is missing just as you are about to leave. You may be asked for a deposit, so make sure you get a receipt for this.

USEFUL WORDS AND PHRASES

agent	un agent	*ajon*
bath (*tub*)	la baignoire	*ben-ywahr*
bathroom	la salle de bain	*sal duh ban*
bedroom	la chambre	*shonbr*
blind	le store	*stor*
blocked	bouché	*booshay*
boiler	le chauffe-eau	*shohff oh*
break	casser	*kassay*
broken	cassé	*kassay*
caretaker	le/la concierge	*konsee-airj*
central heating	le chauffage central	*shohffaj sontrahl*
cleaner	la femme de ménage	*fam duh maynaj*
comforter	la couette	*koo-et*
crib	le lit pour bébé	*lee pour baybay*
deposit	la caution	*kohss-ion*
drain	l'égout	*aygoo*
electrician	l'électricien	*aylektreess-yan*
electricity	l'électricité	*aylektreess-eetay*
faucet	le robinet	*robeenay*
fusebox	la boîte à fusibles	*bwat ah foozeeb-l*
garbage can	la poubelle	*poobel*
gas	le gaz	*gaz*
grill	le gril	*greel*

heater	le radiateur	radee-atur
highchair	la chaise haute	shayz oht
iron	le fer à repasser	fair ah ruhpassay
ironing board	la planche à repasser	plonsh ah ruhpassay
keys	les clés	klay
kitchen	la cuisine	kweezeen
leak (noun)	la fuite	fweet
(verb)	couler	koolay
light	la lumière	loomee-air
light bulb	l'ampoule	onpool
living room	le séjour	sayjoor
maid	la femme de chambre	fam duh shonbr
pillow	l'oreiller	oray-yay
pillowcase	la taie d'oreiller	teh doray-yay
plumber	le plombier	plonb-yay
refrigerator	le frigo	freegoh
refund	le remboursement	ronboorsmon
sheets	les draps	drah
shower	la douche	doosh
sink	le lavabo	lavaboh
stopper	le robinet d'arrêt	robeenay dar-reh
stove	la cuisinière	kweezenee-air
swimming pool	la piscine	peeseen
swimming pool engineer	le technicien responsable de la piscine	tekneess-yan ruhsponsab-l duh la peeseen
toilet	les toilettes	twalet
towel	la serviette	sairvee-et
washing machine	la machine à laver	masheen ah lavay
water	l'eau	oh
water heater	le chauffe-eau	shohff oh

Does the price include gas/electricity/cleaning?
Est-ce que le prix comprend le gaz/l'électricité/le nettoyage?
esskuh luh pree konprond luh gaz/laylektreess-eetay/luh nettwah-yaj

Do I need to sign an inventory?
Est-ce que je dois signer un état des lieux?
esskuh juh dwah seen-yay an ayta day lyuh

Where is this item?
Où se trouve cet objet?
oo suh troov set objay

Please take it off the inventory
Pouvez-vous le retirer de l'état des lieux?
poovay voo luh ruhteeray duh layta day lyuh

We've broken this
Nous avons cassé ceci
nooz avon kassay suhsee

This was broken when we arrived
C'était cassé quand nous sommes arrivés
sayteh kassay kon noo somz arreevay

This was missing when we arrived
Ça n'y était pas quand nous sommes arrivés
sa nyay-teh pa kon noo somz arreevay

Can I have my deposit back?
Puis-je récupérer ma caution?
pweej raykoopayray ma kohss-ion

Can we have an extra bed?
Pourrions-nous avoir un lit supplémentaire?
pooree-on nooz avwahr an lee sooplaymontair

Can we have more dishes/silverware?
Pourrions-nous avoir plus de vaisselle/couverts?
pooree-on nooz avwahr ploo duh vess-el/koovair

Where is …?
Où se trouve …?
oo suh troov

When does the maid come?
Quand vient la femme de chambre?
kon vee-an la fam duh shonbr

Where can I buy/find ...?
Où est-ce que je peux acheter/trouver ...?
oo esskuh juh puh ashuhtay/troovay

How does the water heater work?
Comment est-ce que le chauffe-eau fonctionne?
kommon esskuh luh shohff oh fonkss-ion

Do you do baby-sitting?
Est-ce que vous gardez les enfants?
esskuh voo garday layz onfon

Do you make lunch/dinner?
Est-ce que vous préparez le déjeuner/le dîner?
esskuh voo prayparay luh day-juhnay/luh deenay

Do we have to pay extra or is it included?
Est-ce que nous devons payer un supplément, ou est-ce
  que c'est compris?
esskuh noo duhvon pay-ay an sooplaymon oo eskuh seh kompree

The shower doesn't work
La douche ne marche pas
la doosh nuh marsh pa

The sink is blocked
Le lavabo est bouché
luh lavaboh eh booshay

The sink/toilet is leaking
L'évier/le toilet coule
layvyay/luh vay say kool

There's a burst pipe
Une canalisation a sauté
oon kanaleezass-ion ah sohtay

The garbage has not been collected for a week
Depuis une semaine les ordures n'ont pas été enlevées
duhpwee oon suhmen layz ordoor non paz aytay onluhvay

There's no electricity/gas/water
Il n'y a pas d'électricité/de gaz/d'eau
eel nya pa daylektreess-eetay/duh gaz/doh

The bottled gas has run out—how do we get a new canister?
Il n'y a plus de gaz—comment pouvons-nous obtenir une nouvelle bouteille?
eel nya ploo duh gaz—kommon poovon noo obtuhneer oon noovel bootay

Can you fix it today?
Pouvez-vous le réparer aujourd'hui?
poovay voo luh rayparay ohjoordwee

What is the name and telephone number of the nearest doctor/dentist?
Pouvez-vous me donner le nom et numéro de téléphone du docteur/dentiste le plus proche?
poovay voo muh donnay luh non ay noomayroh duh taylayfon doo doktur/donteest luh ploo prosh

Send your bill to ...
Envoyez votre facture à ...
onvwah-yay vottr faktoor ah

I'm staying at ...
Je suis à...
juh swee

Thanks for looking after us so well
Merci de vous être si bien occupé de nous
mairsee de vooz ettr see byan okoopay duh noo

See you again next year
A l'année prochaine
ah lannay proshen

DRIVING

Drive on the right, pass on the left. A solid line in the center of the road must never be crossed. Passing when there is a solid center line is a serious offense and can result in an on-the-spot fine. A broken center line may be crossed for the purpose of passing another vehicle or for crossing the road. Double lines, one solid and the other broken, may be crossed only where the broken line is immediately to the driver's left. Double lines must not be crossed when the solid line is nearest to the driver's left-hand side.

The horn is used very frequently in France (especially in Paris), even if the **code de la route** (driving regulations) forbids it. Seat belts must be worn at all times.

Speed limits: In built-up areas vehicles must not exceed 31 mph 50 km/h. Some urban areas have a lower speed limit than this, which is indicated at the point where it comes into effect. Outside urban areas the speed limits are as follows: toll highways 81 mph (130 km/h); free highways and dual roadways 68 mph (110 km/h); all other roads outside towns 56 mph (90 km/h). These limits apply also to motorcycles over 81cc; lighter machines (51cc–80cc) are restricted to 46 mph (75 km/h) while mopeds up to 50cc may not travel faster than 28 mph (45 km/h). On wet roads, speed limits are reduced from 68 to 62 mph (130 to 110 km/h), from 81 to 68 mph (110 to 100 km/h), and from 56 to 50 mph (90 to 80 km/h).

Right of way: In built-up areas you must yield to vehicles coming up on your right. On some entrance ramps, you may have the right of way, or you may see a sign saying **vous n'avez pas la priorité** (below the usual entrance symbol in a red triangle), meaning you must yield. Outside built-up areas, your right of way is indicated by **passage protégé** below an intersection sign, or by the broad arrow intersection sign, or by a yellow diamond sign.

Highways: There are two types of highway in France—the **autoroutes de dégagement**, which are found around towns and are free, and the **autoroutes de liaison** or **autoroutes à péage**, which are toll highways. The French highway system is spread over the country and allows quick access to most French **régions**. The most important are: **l'autoroute du Nord** (Paris-Lille), **l'autoroute de l'Est** (Paris-Strasbourg), **l'autoroute du Soleil** (Paris-Marseilles), **la Languedocienne** (Orange-Le Perthus), **l'Aquitaine** (Paris-Bordeaux), and **l'Océane** (Paris-Nantes).

Parking: Drivers must park on the right-hand side of the road in the direction the car is traveling.

In towns, parking is usually restricted between 9 AM and 12:30 PM and 2:30 PM and 7 PM during weekdays. You may have to use a **parcmètre** (parking meter) or pay for parking—**parking payant**. This can mean taking a ticket on arrival and paying on departure. In areas covered by **horodateurs**, you will have to buy a ticket and display it.

Documentation: you must carry the original vehicle registration document, a valid driver's license, and current insurance certificate.

Fines: you can be fined on the spot for: exceeding the drunk driving limit, speeding, and not wearing a seat belt. The police have to issue a receipt for the amount paid.

SOME COMMON ROAD SIGNS

The majority of road signs in France follow international conventions, but you may see the following:

accotement non stabilisé	soft shoulder
aire de croisement	passing place
arrêt interdit	no stopping
autoroute	highway
autoroute à péage	toll highway
autres directions	other directions
brouillard fréquent	risk of fog

→

carrefour dangereux	dangerous intersection
centre-ville	town center
chaussée déformée	uneven road surface
chaussée glissante	slippery road surface
chute de pierres	falling rocks
danger de verglas	danger of black ice
déviation	diversion
douane	customs
école	school
embranchement d'autoroutes	highway junction
entrée interdite	no entry
fin d'autoroute	end of highway
gravillons	loose asphalt
I	tourist information
nids-de-poule	potholes
passage à niveau	grade crossing
passage interdit	no through road
passage protégé	priority road
péage	toll
piétons	pedestrians
poids lourds	heavy vehicles
point noir	accident-prone area
premiers secours	first aid
prudence	caution
ralentir	slow down
rappel	reminder
riverains autorisés	residents only
route barrée	road closed
route départementale	secondary road
route nationale	main road
route verglacée	black ice
sens unique	one-way street
serrez à droite	keep to the right
stationnement à durée limitée	restricted parking
stationnement alterné	parking on alternate sides

→

stationnement interdit	no parking	
toutes directions	all directions	
travaux	road construction	
virage dangereux	dangerous bend	
virages sur … km	bends for … km	
voie pour véhicules lents	slow lane	
zone piétonnière	shopping center	

USEFUL WORDS AND PHRASES

automatic	automatique	*ohtomateek*
brakes	les freins	*fran*
car	la voiture	*vwahtoor*
car ferry	le car ferry	*kar fairree*
clutch	l'embrayage	*onbrayaj*
drive	conduire	*kondweer*
driver's license	le permis de conduire	*permee duh kondweer*
engine	le moteur	*motur*
exhaust	le pot d'échappement	*poh dayshappmon*
fanbelt	la courroie du ventilateur	*koo-rwah doo vonteelatur*
garage *(for repairs)*	le garage	*garraj*
gas	l'essence	*essonss*
gas station	la station-service	*stass-ion sairvees*
gear	la vitesse	*veetess*
headlights	les phares	*far*
highway	l'autoroute	*ohto-root*
hood	le capot	*kapoh*
intersection	le carrefour	*karrfoor*
junction	le croisement	*krwahzmon*
(highway entry)	l'entrée	*ontray*
(highway exit)	la sortie	*sortee*
license plate	la plaque d'immatriculation	*plak deematreekoo-lass-ion*
manual	manuelle	*manoo-el*

mirror	le rétroviseur	*raytroveezur*
motorcycle	la moto	*motoh*
parking lot	le parking	*par-keeng*
(*multi-level*)	le parking à étages	*par-keeng ah aytaj*
road	la route	*root*
skid (*verb*)	déraper	*dayrappay*
spare parts	des pièces de rechange	*pee-ess duh ruhshonj*
spark plug	la bougie	*boojee*
speed	la vitesse	*veetess*
speed limit	vitesse limitée	*veetess leemeetay*
speedometer	le compteur de vitesse	*kontur duh veetess*
steering wheel	le volant	*volon*
taillights	les feux arrière	*fuh arree-air*
tire	le pneu	*p-nuh*
traffic lights	les feux	*fuh*
trailer	la remorque	*ruhmork*
transmission	la boîte de vitesses	*bwat duh veetess*
truck	le camion	*kamion*
trunk	le coffre	*koffr*
turn signal	le clignotant	*kleen-yoton*
van	la camionnette	*kamionet*
vehicle registration documents	la carte grise	*kart greez*
wheel	la roue	*roo*
windshield	le pare-brise	*par breez*
windshield wiper	un essuie-glace	*esswee glass*

I'd like some gas/oil/water
Je voudrais de l'essence/de l'huile/de l'eau
juh voodreh duh lessonss/duh lweel/duh loh

Fill it up, please!
Le plein, s'il vous plaît!
luh plan seel voo pleh

I'd like 35 liters of unleaded
Je voudrais trente-cinq litres de sans plomb
juh voodreh tront sank leetr duh son plon

Do you do repairs?
Faites-vous les réparations?
fet voo lay rayparass-ion

Can you repair the clutch?
Pouvez-vous réparer l'embrayage?
poovay voo rayparay lonbrayaj

How long will it take?
Combien de temps est-ce que ça prendra?
konbyan duh ton esskuh sa prondra

Can you repair it today?
Pouvez-vous le réparer aujourd'hui?
poovay voo luh rayparay ohjoordwee

There is something wrong with the engine
Le moteur ne fonctionne pas bien
luh motur nuh fonkss-ion pa byan

The engine is overheating
Le moteur chauffe
luh motur shohf

I need a new tire
Je voudrais un pneu neuf
juh voodreh an p-nuh nuhf

Can you replace this?
Pouvez-vous remplacer ceci?
poovay voo ronplassay suhsee

The turn signal is not working
Le clignotant ne fonctionne pas
luh kleen-yoton nuh fonkss-ion pa

Is there a parking lot near here?
Est-ce qu'il y a un parking dans les environs?
esskeel-ya an par-keeng don layz onveeron

Can I park here?
Est-ce que je peux me garer ici?
esskuh juh puh muh garray ee-see

Do I have to pay?
Faut-il payer?
fohteel payay

I'd like to rent a car
Je voudrais louer une voiture
juh voodreh loo-ay oon vwahtoor

I'd like an automatic/a manual
J'aimerais une voiture à transmission automatique/manuelle
jemmereh oon vwahtoor ah tronsmeess-ion ohtomateek/manoo-el

How much is it for one day?
Ça coûte combien pour une journée?
sa koot konbyan poor oon joornay

Is there a mileage charge?
Est-ce qu'il y a des frais de kilométrage?
esskeel-ya day freh duh keelomaytraj

Can we rent a baby/child seat?
Pouvons-nous louer un siège pour bébé/enfant?
poovon noo looay an seeayj poor baybay/onfon

When do I have to return it?
Quand est-ce que je dois la ramener?
kont esskuh juh dwah la ramuhnay

Where is the nearest garage?
Pouvez-vous m'indiquer le garage le plus proche?
poovay voo mandeekay luh garraj luh ploo prosh

How do I get to ...?
Comment va-t-on à ...?
komm<u>on</u> vat <u>on</u> ah

Is this the road to ...?
Est-ce que c'est bien la route pour ...?
esskuh seh by<u>an</u> la root poor

Which is the quickest way to ...?
Quelle est la voie la plus rapide pour arriver à ...?
kell eh la vwah la pl<u>oo</u> rapeed poor arreevay ah

DIRECTIONS YOU MAY BE GIVEN

à droite	right
à gauche	left
au prochain carrefour	at the next intersection
avancez	go forward
deuxième à gauche	second on the left
passez ...	go past ...
première à droite	first on the right
reculez	reverse
tournez à droite/gauche	turn right/left
tout droit	straight ahead

THINGS YOU'LL SEE

aire de repos	rest area
aire de service	service area
aire de stationnement	parking area
arrêtez votre moteur	turn off engine
attendez ici	wait here
cire pour voiture	car wax
eau	water
essence	gas

→

gas-oil	diesel
horodateur	pay and display
huile	oil
lavage du pare-brise	windshield washer
monnaie exacte	exact change
parcmètre	parking meter
parking	parking lot
parking à étages	multi-level parking lot
parking payant	paying parking lot
parking surveillé	parking lot with attendant
prenez un ticket	take a ticket
pression de l'air	air pressure
pression des pneus	tire pressure
réparations	repairs
réservé aux clients	patrons only
roulez au pas	drive at walking pace
sans plomb	unleaded
sortie	exit
station-service	gas station
super	leaded gas

THINGS YOU'LL HEAR

Voulez-vous une voiture à transmission automatique ou à transmission manuelle ?
Would you like an automatic or a manual?

Puis-je voir votre permis de conduire ?
May I see your license?

Puis-je voir votre passeport ?
May I see your passport?

TRAVELING AROUND

AIR TRAVEL

Paris has two international airports, Orly and Charles de
Gaulle at Roissy. Both are connected to the main terminals and
train stations in Paris by **navettes** (airport buses). There's also
a train service to Charles de Gaulle, the fast **RER**, which connects
with a free shuttle bus to the air terminal.

CROSSING THE CHANNEL

As well as the Channel Tunnel, many companies run car ferry
and hovercraft services across the Channel. There are also car
ferries to Corsica from Marseilles, Toulon, and Nice.

There are many opportunities for boat trips and do-it-yourself
cruises on the rivers and canals of France, including areas such
as Burgundy, Brittany, and Alsace, among others.

TRAIN TRAVEL

The French trains (**SNCF**) are both fast and punctual, and
have two classes, first and second. International trains connect
Paris with most parts of Europe, while fast, regular Inter-City
and express services link the main French towns. The main
types of train are:

TGV (Train à Grande Vitesse): high-speed train.
Rapide: fast Inter-City train, often named (l'Aquitaine,
le Drapeau, l'Etendard, le Mistral, etc).
Express: an ordinary fast train.

You may see the sign **supplément modulé**, which means that
you have to pay a supplement if traveling on a Friday or the
day before a national holiday. Reservations are essential on the
TGV train, and it is compulsory to buy **une résa** (reservation
ticket) with your ticket, both of which you must date-stamp
on the day of use. Look for a machine with the sign **compostez**

votre billet (stamp your ticket). If you buy any train ticket in France (rather than book it before you get there), you must validate this by inserting it into one of the orange-colored machines at the platform entrance. If you don't date-stamp it like this, you may be fined by a roving ticket inspector.

BUS

In the country, buses link mainline train stations with most towns and villages not served by trains. Tickets are available at **tabac-journaux** (newsstands) and—as in Paris, where the same tickets or passes can be used either on the **métro** or on the bus—fares are calculated by distance, one ticket for one fare stage. You must date-stamp your ticket in the machine on the bus—you will see the sign: **oblitérez votre ticket** (punch your ticket). Long-distance bus services are rare in France, but there are sightseeing package tours by bus.

SUBWAY AND SUBURBAN TRAINS

In Paris, the **métro** (subway) is the fastest and most economical way to travel. It's a one-price service regardless of distance, and trains run from about 5:30 AM to 12:30 AM. Tickets are cheapest when bought in booklets of ten (**carnet**), and you can also buy special tourist tickets (inquire at **métro** or train stations, or at any Office de Tourisme in Paris). Lille, Lyons, and Marseilles also have **métro** systems.

There is an extensive suburban train system in Paris—RER (**Réseau Express Régional**)—operated jointly by the SNCF and Paris transport.

TAXI

Taxis are clearly marked and can be hailed or picked up at a stand (there's usually one at the train station). If the taxi has no meter, or if you are going some distance out of town, check the fare beforehand.

Useful Words and Phrases

adult	un adulte	*ad__oo__lt*
airport	l'aéroport	*ah-ayropor*
airport bus	la navette de l'aéroport	*navet duh lah-ayropor*
aisle seat	une place côté couloir	*plass kohtay koolwahr*
baggage claim	le retrait des bagages	*ruhtray day bagaj*
boarding pass	la carte d'embarquement	*kart d__on__barkuhm__on__*
boat	le bateau	*battoh*
buffet	le buffet de la gare	*b__oo__fay duh la gar*
bus	le bus	*b__oo__ss*
bus station	la gare routière	*gar rootee-air*
bus stop	un arrêt de bus	*array duh b__oo__ss*
carry-on luggage	les bagages à main	*bagaj ah m__an__*
check-in desk	l'enregistrement des bagages	*__on__ruhjeestruh-m__on__ day bagaj*
child	un enfant	*__on__f__on__*
compartment	le compartiment	*k__on__parteem__on__*
connection	la correspondance	*korresp__on__-d__on__ss*
cruise	la croisière	*krwahzee-air*
customs	la douane	*doo-wan*
departure lounge	la salle d'embarquement	*sal d__on__barkm__on__*
dining car	le wagon-restaurant	*vagon restor__on__*
domestic arrivals	arrivées intérieures	*arreevay __antayree-ur__*
domestic departures	départs intérieurs	*daypar __antayree-ur__*
entrance	l'entrée	*__on__tray*
excess baggage	l'excédent de bagages	*eksaid__on__ duh bagaj*
exit	la sortie	*sortee*
fare	le prix du ticket	*pree d__oo__ teekay*
ferry	le ferry	*fairree*
first class	première classe	*pruhmee-air klass*
flight	le vol	*vol*

48

flight number	le numéro du vol	*noomayroh doo vol*
gate	la porte	*port*
hovercraft	un hovercraft,	*ovairkraft,*
	un aéroglisseur	*ah-ayrohgleesur*
hoverport	un hoverport	*ovairpor*
hydrofoil	un hydrofoil,	*eedro-foyl,*
	un hydroptère	*eedroptair*
international	arrivées	*arreevay*
arrivals	internationales	*antairnass-ionahl*
international	départs	*daypar*
departures	internationaux	*antairnass-ionoh*
long-distance bus	un car	*un kar*
lost and found	le bureau des objets	*booroh dayz objay*
	trouvés	*troovay*
luggage cart	un chariot	*sharee-oh*
luggage storage	la consigne	*konseen*
room		
nonsmoking	non-fumeurs	*non foomur*
number 5 bus	le bus numéro 5	*booss noomayroh*
		sank
one-way	un aller simple	*allay sanp-l*
passport	un passeport	*passpor*
platform	le quai	*kay*
port	le port	*por*
round-trip ticket	un aller retour	*allay-ruhtoor*
seat	une place	*plass*
second class	seconde	*segond*
sleeper car	un wagon-lit	*vagon lee*
smoking	fumeurs	*foomur*
station	la gare	*gar*
(*subway*)	la station	*stass-ion*
subway	le métro	*maytroh*
taxi	un taxi	*taxee*
terminal	le terminus	*tairmeenoos*
ticket (*air, train*)	un billet	*bee-yay*
(*bus, subway*)	un ticket	*teekay*

ticket office	le guichet	*gheeshay*
timetable	l'horaire	*orrair*
train	le train	*tran*
train station	le chemin de fer	*shuhman duh fai*
transit system map	un plan du réseau	*plon doo rayzoh*
underground passage	un passage souterrain	*passaj sootairran*
waiting room	la salle d'attente	*sal dattont*
window seat (*air*)	une place côté hublot	*plass kohtay oobloh*
(*train*)	une place côté fenêtre	*plass kohtay fuhnettr*

AIR TRAVEL

I'd like a nonsmoking seat, please
Je voudrais une place en non-fumeurs, s'il vous plaît
juh voodreh oon plass on non foomur seel voo pleh

I'd like a window seat, please
Je voudrais une place côté hublot, s'il vous plaît
juh voodreh oon plass kohtay oobloh seel voo pleh

How long will the flight be delayed?
Combien l'avion aura-t-il de retard ?
konbyan lav-ion oh-ratteel duh ruhtar

Which gate for the flight to …?
Quelle porte pour le vol à destination de …?
kell port poor luh vol ah desteenass-ion duh …

TRAIN, BUS, AND SUBWAY TRAVEL

When does the train/bus for Paris leave/arrive?
A quelle heure part/arrive le train/bus pour Paris?
ah kell ur par/arreev luh tran/booss poor paree

When is the next train/bus to Lyons?
A quelle heure part le prochain train/bus pour Lyon?
ah kell ur par luh proshan tran/booss poor lee-on

When is the first/last train/bus to Grenoble?
A quelle heure part le premier/dernier train/bus pour Grenoble?
ah kell ur par luh pruhm-yay/dairn-yay tran/booss poor gruhnob-l

What is the fare to Nantes?
Quelle est le prix du billet pour Nantes?
kell eh luh pree doo bee-yay poor nont

Do I have to change trains/buses?
Faut-il changer de train/bus?
foh-teel shonjay duh tran/booss

Does the train/bus stop at Rouen?
Est-ce que le train/bus s'arrête à Rouen?
esskuh luh tran/booss sarret ah roo-on

How long does it take to get to Bordeaux?
Combien de temps faut-il pour aller à Bordeaux?
konbyan duh ton foh-teel poor allay ah bordoh

Where can I buy a ticket?
Où est-ce que je peux acheter un billet?
oo esskuh juh puh ashtay an bee-yay

A one-way/round-trip ticket to Strasbourg, please
Un aller simple/aller retour Strasbourg, s'il vous plaît
an allay sanp-l/allay-ruhtoor strazboorg seel voo pleh

Could you help me get a ticket?
Pouvez-vous m'aider à obtenir un billet?
poovay voo mayday ah obtuhneer an bee-yay

Do I have to pay a supplement?
Est-ce qu'il y a un supplément à payer?
esskeel-ya an sooplaymon ah pay-ay

I'd like to reserve a seat
Je voudrais réserver une place
juh voodreh rayzairvay oon plass

Is this the right train/bus for Montpellier?
Est-ce bien le train/bus pour Montpellier?
ess by_an luh tr_an/bo_oss poor m_onpailee-yay

Is this the right platform for the Nice train?
Est-ce bien le quai pour le train qui va à Nice?
ess by_an le kay poor luh tr_an kee va ah neess

Which platform for the Lille train?
De quel quai part le train pour Lille?
duh kell kay par luh tr_an poor leel

Is the train/bus late?
Est-ce que le train/bus a du retard?
esskuh luh tr_an/bo_oss ah d_oo ruhtar

Is this a nonsmoking compartment?
Ce compartiment est-il non-fumeurs?
suh k_onpartee-m_on eteel n_on fo_omur

Is this seat free?
Est-ce que cette place est libre?
esskuh set plass eh leebr

This seat is taken
Cette place est occupée
set plass et okk_oopay

I have reserved this seat
J'ai réservé cette place
jay rayzairvay set plass

May I open/close the window?
Est-ce que je peux ouvrir/fermer la fenêtre?
esskuh juh puh oovreer/fairmay la fuhn-ettr

When do we arrive in Toulouse?
Savez-vous à quelle heure nous arrivons à Toulouse?
savay voo ah kell ur nooz arreev_on ah toolooz

What station is this?
Quelle est cette gare?
kell eh set gar

Do we stop at Metz?
Est-ce que le train/bus s'arrête à Metz?
esskuh luh tran/booss sarret ah metz

Is there a dining car on this train?
Est-ce qu'il y a un wagon-restaurant dans ce train?
esskeel-ya an vagon restoron don suh tran

Where is the nearest subway station?
Pouvez-vous m'indiquer la station de métro la plus proche?
poovay voo mandeekay la stass-ion duh maytroh la ploo prosh

THINGS YOU'LL HEAR

Le prochain train part à …
The next train leaves at …

Changez à …
Change at …

Vous devez payer un supplément
You must pay a supplement

Il n'y a plus de places disponibles pour …
There are no more seats available on …

Which buses go to the city center?
Quels sont les bus qui vont au centre-ville?
kell son lay booss kee von oh sontr veel

How often do the buses to Bourg-en-Bresse run?
Quelle est la fréquence des bus pour Bourg-en-Bresse?
kell eh la fraykonss day booss poor boorg-on-bress

Will you let me know when we're there?
Pourriez-vous me faire savoir quand nous y serons?
pooree-ay voo muh fair savwahr k<u>on</u> nooz ee suhr<u>on</u>

Do I have to get off yet?
Est-ce que je dois descendre maintenant?
ess kuh juh dwa days<u>on</u>dr m<u>a</u>tn<u>on</u>

Do you go near the Musée d'Orsay?
Passez-vous près du Musée d'Orsay?
passay voo preh d<u>oo</u> m<u>oo</u>zay dorsay

Taxi

Can you let me off here?
Pouvez-vous me déposer ici?
poovay voo muh daypozay ee-see

How much is it to the station?
Combien ça coûte pour aller à la gare?
k<u>on</u>by<u>an</u> sa koot poor allay ah la gar

Could you wait here for me and take me back?
Pourriez-vous m'attendre ici et me ramener?
pooree-ay voo matt<u>on</u>dr ee-see ay muh ramuhnay

Things You'll See

accès aux quais/trains	to the platforms/trains
aérogare	air terminal
aéroglisseur	hovercraft
annuler	cancel
appuyez ici	press here
arrêt de bus	bus stop
arrêt facultatif	request stop
arrivée(s)	arrival(s)
banlieue	suburbs

→

billeterie automatique	ticket machine
billets	tickets
carnet	book of tickets
carte	pass
carte de réduction	pass enabling you to buy a reduced-rate rail ticket
cet appareil ne rend pas la monnaie	this machine does not give change
change	currency exchange
compostez votre billet	stamp your ticket
consigne	luggage storage
consigne automatique	luggage lockers
contrôle des bagages	baggage claim
cordon d'alarme	emergency cord
correspondance	transfers, connection
départ(s)	departure(s)
dessert ...	stops at ...
dimanches et jours fériés	on Sundays and public holidays
douane	customs
embarquement	boarding
enfants	children
entrée	entrance
entrée à l'avant/à l'arrière	entry at the front/rear
entrée interdite	no entry
Express	ordinary fast train
femmes	women (bathroom)
fermeture automatique des portes	doors close automatically
fumeurs	smoking
gare	station
grandes lignes	main lines
guichet	ticket office
heure	time
hommes	men (bathroom)
horaire	timetable
hydroptère	hydrofoil

→

interdit aux voyageurs	staff only
introduire ici	insert here
issue de secours	emergency exit
journées à tarif réduit	inexpensive travel days
jours de semaine uniquement	weekdays only
libre	vacant
livraison des bagages	baggage claim
navette de l'aéroport	airport bus
ne pas se pencher par la fenêtre	do not lean out of the window
non-fumeurs	no smoking
n'oubliez pas de composter votre billet	don't forget to validate your ticket
oblitérez votre billet	punch your ticket
occupé	occupied
ouverture	opening
passage interdit	no entry
passager(s)	passenger(s)
passage souterrain	underground passage
payez ici	pay here
pénalité pour abus	penalty for misuse
pièce(s)	coin(s)
pièces rejetées	reject coins
place (assise)	seat
plan de métro	subway map
plan du réseau	transit system map
plein tarif	full price
porte	gate
pour faire votre choix, appuyez sur l'écran	to make your selection, touch the screen
poussez	push
quai	platform; dock
rame	train
Rapide	intercity train
relevez	lift up

$\longrightarrow$

renseignements	inquiries
RER	Paris suburban rail system
résa	reservation ticket on TGV
réservé	reserved
réservé au personnel	staff only
retard/retardé	delay/delayed
salle d'attente	waiting room
sans issue	no exit
satellite	section of airport terminal
SNCF	French Trains
sortie	exit
sortie de secours	emergency exit
station de métro	subway station
station de taxis	taxi stand
tabac-journaux	newsstand
TGV	high-speed train
ticket de quai	platform ticket
ticket ou carnet de métro	métro ticket or book of tickets
tirez	pull
titre de transport	ticket
tous les jours sauf ...	every day except ...
train à supplément	train for which you must pay a supplement
voie	platform, track
voiture	car, coach
vol direct	direct flight
vols intérieurs	domestic flights
wagon-lit	sleeper
wagon-restaurant	dining car

THINGS YOU'LL HEAR

Avez-vous des bagages?
Do you have any luggage?

Fumeurs ou non-fumeurs?
Smoking or nonsmoking?

Place côté hublot ou côte couloir?
Window seat or aisle seat?

Prière de vous rendre maintenant à la porte numéro quatre
Please proceed to gate number four

Les billets, s'il vous plaît
Tickets, please

Attention au départ
The train is about to leave

Le train à destination de Paris partira de la voie 4 dans 10 minutes
The train for Paris will leave from platform 4 in 10 minutes

Le train en provenance de Rennes arrivera à la voie 5 dans 15 minutes
The train from Rennes will arrive at platform 5 in 15 minutes

Le train en provenance de Bordeaux a un retard de 17 minutes
The train from Bordeaux is running 17 minutes late

Préparez vos billets, s'il vous plaît
Have your tickets ready, please

Ouvrez vos valises, s'il vous plaît
Open your suitcases, please

EATING OUT

It is not difficult to eat well and inexpensively in France. Since prices have to be displayed, by law, in the window of an eating establishment, you can readily fit your choice of restaurant to your budget. Although service is included in the bill, it is customary to leave a tip for the waiter or waitress. In cafés, even if you have just popped in for coffee or a drink, it is traditional to leave the leftover coins from your change.

Every town has a number of cafés where, at lunchtime, you can order a simple sandwich, a **croque-monsieur** (a grilled ham and cheese sandwich which, with the addition of an egg, becomes a **croque-madame**), the **plat du jour** (dish of the day), **rillettes** (pork or goose meat minced very finely so that it can be spread on bread), pâté, or a platter of crudités or cold meats.

Bistros are small bars, often family-run, that also sometimes serve a selection of traditional dishes or snacks at lunchtime and in the evening. The **menu du jour** (today's menu) is usually a good value. Regional specialties that you may encounter include: **crêpes** in Brittany; **choucroute** (sauerkraut with sausages and pieces of smoked ham) and onion tart in Alsace; **ratatouille** in Provence; and **bouillabaisse** (fish soup) and **salade niçoise** (mixed salad containing olives, anchovies, tuna, tomatoes, and other vegetables) around the Mediterranean coast. House wine is available in carafes, but if you prefer your wine by the bottle, you will find a few listed on the menu.

Brasseries are often large and noisy—not the place to go for an intimate dinner—and offer beer on tap as well as wine. They stay open late, and snacks and full meals are usually available at any time.

If you are planning a picnic, **charcuteries** offer a wide range of take-out food, such as sausages, pâté, ham, quiche, and a nice variety of salads. Some of the items offered that may not be readily identifiable are: **andouille** (a cold sausage made from pig's or calf's intestines); **boudin blanc** (white pudding); **crépinette** (a small sausage patty wrapped in fat); **fromage de** tête (head-cheese); **poitrine fumée** (smoked bacon); and **rillettes** (a pâté made from pork). The difference between a **saucisse** and a **saucisson** is that the former is fresh and eaten warm, the latter dried and eaten cold.

French cafés and bars always sell coffee. If you ask for **un café** or **un expresso**, you'll get a small, black coffee. **Un crème** is a small coffee with milk and **un grand crème** is a large coffee with milk. You can also ask for **un café léger** (weak coffee) or **un café bien serré** (very strong coffee).

USEFUL WORDS AND PHRASES

appetizer	une entrée	_ontray_
beer	de la bière	_bee-air_
bottle	une bouteille	_bootay_
bread	du pain	_pan_
butter	du beurre	_bur_
café	un café	_kaffay_
cake	du gâteau	_gattoh_
carafe	une carafe	_karaff_
check	l'addition	_addeess-ion_
chef	le chef	_shef_
child's portion	une portion enfant	_porss-ion onfon_
coffee	du café	_kaffay_
cup	une tasse	_tass_
dessert	un dessert	_daissair_
fork	une fourchette	_foorshet_
glass	un verre	_vair_
half-liter	un demi-litre	_duhmee leettr_
knife	un couteau	_kootoh_
main course	le plat principal	_pla pranseepal_
menu	le menu	_muhnoo_
milk	du lait	_leh_
napkin	une serviette	_sairvee-et_
pepper	du poivre	_pwahvr_
plate	une assiette	_assee-et_

receipt	le reçu	*ruhss<u>oo</u>*
restaurant	le restaurant	*restohr<u>on</u>*
salt	du sel	*sel*
sandwich	un sandwich	*s<u>on</u>dweech*
snack	un snack	*'snack'*
soup	de la soupe	*soop*
spoon	une cuillère	*kwee-air*
sugar	du sucre	*s<u>oo</u>kr*
table	une table	*tabb-l*
tea	du thé	*tay*
teaspoon	une cuillère à café	*kwee-air ah kaffay*
tip	un pourboire	*poorbwahr*
waiter	un serveur	*sairvur*
waitress	une serveuse	*sairvuhz*
water	de l'eau	*oh*
wine	du vin	*v<u>an</u>*
wine list	la carte des vins	*kart day v<u>an</u>*

A table for one, please
Une table pour une personne, s'il vous plaît
<u>oo</u>n tabb-l poor <u>oo</u>n pairson seel voo pleh

A table for two/three, please
Une table pour deux/trois personnes, s'il vous plaît
<u>oo</u>n tabb-l poor duh/trwah pairson seel voo pleh

Is there a highchair?
Auriez-vous une chaise haute?
oriayvoo oon shayz oht

Can we see the menu/wine list?
Le menu/la carte des vins, s'il vous plaît
luh muhn<u>oo</u>/la kart day v<u>an</u> seel voo pleh

What would you recommend?
Que recommandez-vous?
kuh ruhkomm<u>on</u>day voo

I'd like …
J'aimerais …
jemmereh

Just a cup of coffee/tea, please
Un café/thé seulement
<u>an</u> *kaffay/tay suhlm<u>on</u>*

I only want a snack
Je voudrais juste manger un snack
juh voodreh <u>joost</u> m<u>on</u>jay <u>an</u> snack

Is there a fixed price menu?
Est-ce qu'il y a un menu du jour?
esskeel-ya <u>an</u> muhn<u>oo</u> doo joor

A carafe of house red, please
Une carafe de vin rouge maison, s'il vous plaît
<u>oon</u> *karaff duh v<u>an</u> rooj mezz<u>on</u> seel voo pleh*

Do you have any vegetarian dishes?
Est-ce que vous servez des plats végétariens?
esskuh voo sairvay day pla vayjaytary<u>an</u>

Could we have some water?
Est-ce que nous pourrions avoir de l'eau?
esskuh noo pooree-<u>on</u> avwahr duh loh

Do you serve children's portions?
Est-ce que vous servez des portions enfant?
esskuh voo sairvay day porss-i<u>on</u> <u>onfon</u>

Can you warm this bottle/baby food for me?
Pourriez-vous réchauffer ce biberon/petit pot pour moi?
pooreeay voo rayshohfay suh beebuhron/puhteepoh poor mwah

Waiter/waitress!
Garçon/Mademoiselle!
garss<u>on</u>/madmwazel

We didn't order this
Ce n'est pas ce que nous avons commandé
sneh pa suh kuh nooz avon kommonday

You've forgotten to bring my dessert
Vous avez oublié d'apporter mon dessert
vooz avay ooblee-ay dapportay mon daissair

May we have some more …?
Est-ce qu'on peut avoir plus de …?
esskon puh avwahr ploo duh

Can I have another knife/fork?
Est-ce que je peux avoir un autre couteau/une autre fourchette?
esskuh juh puh avwahr an oht-r kootoh/oon oht-r foorshet

May we have the check, please?
L'addition, s'il vous plaît
laddeess-ion seel voo pleh

Could I have a receipt, please?
Est-ce que je peux avoir un reçu, s'il vous plaît?
esskuh juh puh avwahr an ruhssoo seel voo pleh

Can we pay separately?
Est-ce que nous pouvons payer séparément?
esskuh noo poovon pay-ay sayparaymon

The meal was very good, thank you
C'était très bon, merci
sayteh treh bon mairsee

THINGS YOU'LL HEAR

Bon appétit!
Enjoy your meal!

Que désirez-vous boire?
What would you like to drink?

MENU GUIDE

abats	offal
abricot	apricot
à emporter	to carry out
agneau	lamb
aiguillette de bœuf	slices of rump steak
ail	garlic
ailloli	garlic mayonnaise
à la broche	roasted on a spit
à la jardinière	with assorted vegetables
à la normande	in cream sauce
alose	shad (fish)
amande	almond
ananas	pineapple
anchois	anchovies
andouillette	spicy sausage
anguille	eel
à point	medium
araignée de mer	spider crab
artichaut	artichoke
asperge	asparagus
aspic de volaille	chicken in aspic
assiette anglaise	selection of cold meats
au gratin	baked in a milk, cream, and cheese sauce
au vin blanc	in white wine
avocat	avocado
baba au rhum	rum baba
banane	banana
bananes flambées	bananas flambéed in brandy
barbue	brill (fish)
bavaroise	light mousse
béarnaise	with béarnaise sauce (thick sauce made with eggs and butter)
bécasse	woodcock
béchamel	white sauce, **béchamel** sauce
beignet	fritter, doughnut
beignet aux pommes	apple fritter
betterave	beets
beurre	butter
beurre d'anchois	anchovy paste

beurre d'estragon	butter with tarragon
beurre noir	dark melted butter
bien cuit	well done
bière	beer
bière à la pression	draft beer
bière blonde	lager
bière brune	bitter, dark beer
bière panachée	shandy (beer and lemonade drink)
bifteck	steak
bifteck de cheval	horsemeat steak
biscuit de Savoie	sponge cake
bisque d'écrevisses	crayfish soup
bisque de homard	lobster soup
blanc de blancs	white wine from white grapes
blanquette de veau	veal stew
bleu	rare
bleu d'auvergne	blue cheese from Auvergne
bœuf	beef
bœuf à la ficelle	beef cooked in stock
bœuf bourguignon	beef cooked in red wine
bœuf braisé	braised beef
bœuf en daube	beef casserole
bœuf miroton	beef and onion stew
bœuf mode	beef stew with carrots
bolet	boletus (mushroom)
bouchée à la reine	veal vol-au-vent
boudin blanc	white pudding
boudin noir	black pudding
bouillabaisse	fish soup from the Midi
bouilli	boiled
bouillon	broth
bouillon de légumes	vegetable stock
bouillon de poule	chicken stock
boulette	meatball
bouquet rose	shrimp
bourride	fish soup
braisé	braised
brandade	cod in cream and garlic
brioche	round roll
brochet	pike
brochette	kabob

brugnon	nectarine
brûlot	flambéed brandy
brut	very dry
cabillaud	cod
café	coffee (black)
café au lait	white coffee
café complet	continental breakfast
café crème	white coffee
café glacé	iced coffee
café liégeois	iced coffee with cream
caille	quail
cake	fruitcake
calamar/calmar	squid
calvados	apple brandy
camomille	camomile tea
canapé	small open-faced sandwich, canapé
canard	duck
canard à l'orange	duck in orange sauce
canard aux cerises	duck with cherries
canard aux navets	duck with turnips
canard laqué	Peking duck
canard rôti	roasted duck
caneton	duckling
cantal	white cheese from Auvergne
carbonnade	beef cooked in beer
cari	curry
carotte	carrot
carottes Vichy	carrots in butter and parsley
carpe	carp
carré d'agneau	rack of lamb
carrelet	plaice
carte	menu
carte des vins	wine list
casse-croûte	snacks
cassis	black currant
cassoulet	bean, pork, and duck casserole
céleri	celeriac
céleri en branches	celery
céleri rave	celeriac
céleri rémoulade	celeriac in **rémoulade** dressing
cèpe	cep (mushroom)

cerise	cherry
cerises à l'eau de vie	cherries in brandy
cervelle	brains
chabichou	goat's and cow's milk cheese
chablis	dry white wine from Burgundy
chambré	at room temperature
champignon	mushroom
champignon de Paris	white button mushroom
champignons à la grecque	dish of mushrooms in olive oil, herbs, and tomatoes, served hot or cold
chanterelle	chanterelle (mushroom)
chantilly	whipped cream
charcuterie	sausages, ham, and pâtés; pork products
charlotte	dessert consisting of layers of fruit, cream, and finger biscuits
chasselas	white grape
chausson aux pommes	apple turnover
cheval	horse
chèvre	goat's cheese
chevreuil	venison
chicorée	endive
chiffonnade d'oseille	seasoned sorrel cooked in butter
chocolat chaud	hot chocolate
chocolat glacé	iced chocolate
chou	cabbage
chou à la crème	cream puff
choucroute	sauerkraut with sausages and pieces of smoked ham
chou-fleur	cauliflower
chou-fleur au gratin	cauliflower with cheese
chou rouge	red cabbage
choux de Bruxelles	Brussels sprouts
cidre	cider
cidre doux	sweet cider
citron	lemon
citron pressé	fresh lemon juice
civet de lièvre	jugged hare
clafoutis	baked batter pudding with fruit
cochon de lait	suckling pig
cocktail de crevettes	prawn cocktail
cœur	heart

coing	quince
colin	hake
compote	stewed fruit, compote
comté	hard cheese from the Jura
concombre	cucumber
confit de canard	duck preserved in fat
confit d'oie	goose preserved in fat
confiture	jam
congre	conger eel
consommé	clear soup made from meat or chicken
coq au vin	chicken in red wine
coque	cockle
coquelet	cockerel
coquille Saint-Jacques	scallop served in cream sauce
côte de porc	pork chop
côtelette	chop
cotriade bretonne	fish soup from Brittany
coulommiers	rich, soft cheese
coupe	dessert dish
court-bouillon	stock for poaching fish or meat
couscous	steamed grains of semolina with meat and vegetable stew
crabe	crab
crème	cream, creamy sauce, or dessert; white coffee
crème à la vanille	vanilla custard
crème anglaise	custard
crème chantilly	whipped cream
crème d'asperges	cream of asparagus soup
crème de bolets	cream of mushroom soup
crème de volaille	cream of chicken soup
crème d'huîtres	cream of oyster soup
crème fouettée	whipped cream
crème pâtissière	rich creamy custard
crème renversée	set custard
crème vichyssoise	cold potato and leek soup
crêpe	pancake
crêpe à la béchamel	pancake with **béchamel** sauce
crêpe à la chantilly	pancake with whipped cream
crêpe à la confiture	pancake with jam
crêpe à la crème de marron	pancake with chestnut cream

crêpe à l'œuf	pancake with fried egg
crêpe au chocolat	pancake with chocolate sauce
crêpe au jambon	pancake with ham
crêpe aux fruits de mer	pancake with seafood
crêpe de froment	wheat pancake
crêpes aux champignons	mushroom pancakes
crêpes aux épinards	spinach pancakes
crêpes Suzette	pancakes flambéed with orange sauce
crépinette	small sausage patty wrapped in fat
cresson	cress
crevette grise	shrimp
crevette rose	prawn
croque-madame	grilled cheese and ham sandwich with a fried egg
croque-monsieur	grilled cheese and ham sandwich
crottin de Chavignol	small goat's cheese
crudités	selection of salads, chopped raw vegetables
crustacés	shellfish
cuisses de grenouille	frogs' legs
cuissot de chevreuil	haunch of venison
dartois	pastry with jam
dégustation	(wine) tasting
déjeuner	lunch
digestif	liqueur
dinde	turkey
dîner	dinner
doux	sweet
eau minérale	mineral water
eau minérale gazeuse/plate	sparkling/still mineral water
échalote	shallot
écrevisse	saltwater crayfish
écrevisses à la nage	crayfish in wine and vegetable sauce
endive	chicory, endive
endives au jambon	endives with ham baked in the oven
en papillote	baked in foil or paper
entrecôte	rib steak
entrecôte au poivre	peppered rib steak
entrecôte maître d'hôtel	steak with butter and parsley
entrée	appetizer
entremets	dessert
épaule d'agneau farcie	stuffed shoulder of lamb

éperlan	smelt (fish)
épinards à la crème	spinach with cream
épinards en branches	leaf spinach
escalope à la crème	escalope in cream sauce
escalope de veau milanaise	veal escalope with tomato sauce
escalope panée	breaded escalope
escargot	snail
esquimau	ice cream on a stick
estouffade de bœuf	beef casserole
faisan	pheasant
farci	stuffed
fenouil	fennel
filet	fillet
filet de bœuf Rossini	fillet of beef with **foie gras**
filet de perche	perch fillet
fine	fine brandy
flageolets	kidney beans
flambé	flambéed
flan	custard tart
foie de veau	veal liver
foie gras	goose or duck liver preserve
foies de volaille	chicken livers
fonds d'artichaut	artichoke hearts
fondue bourguignonne	meat fondue
fondue savoyarde	cheese fondue
fraise	strawberry
fraise des bois	wild strawberry
framboise	raspberry
frisée	curly lettuce
frit	deep-fried
frites	french fries
fromage	cheese
fromage blanc	cream cheese
fromage de chèvre	goat's cheese
fruité	fruity
fruits de mer	seafood
galette	round, flat cake or a savory wholemeal crêpe
garni	with potatoes and vegetables
gâteau	cake
gaufre	wafer; waffle
gelée	gelatin

génoise	sponge cake
Gewürztraminer	dry white wine from Alsace
gibelotte de lapin	rabbit stewed in white wine
gibier	game
gigot d'agneau	leg of lamb
gigue de chevreuil	haunch of venison
girolle	chanterelle (mushroom)
glace	ice cream
goujon	gudgeon (fish)
grand cru	vintage wine
gras-double	tripe
gratin	baked cheese dish with milk and cream
gratin dauphinois	layers of sliced potatoes baked in milk, cream, and cheese
gratin de langoustines	scampi au gratin
gratin de queues d'écrevisse	crayfish tails au gratin
gratinée	baked onion soup
grillé	broiled
grive	thrush
grondin	gurnard (fish)
groseille blanche	white currant
groseille rouge	red currant
hachis parmentier	shepherd's pie
hareng mariné	marinated herring
haricots	beans
haricots blancs	haricot beans
haricots verts	green beans
homard	lobster
homard à l'américaine	lobster with tomatoes and white wine
hors-d'œuvre	appetizer
huître	oyster
îles flottantes	floating islands (poached egg whites on top of custard)
infusion	herb tea
jambon	ham
jambon au madère	ham in Madeira wine
jambon de Bayonne	smoked and cured ham
jarret de veau	shin of veal
julienne	soup with chopped vegetables
jus de pomme	apple juice
jus d'orange	orange juice

kir	white wine with black currant liqueur
kirsch	cherry brandy
kugelhof	cake from Alsace
lait	milk
lait grenadine	milk with grenadine cordial
laitue	lettuce
langouste	freshwater crayfish
langoustine	scampi
langue de bœuf	ox tongue
lapereau	young rabbit
lapin	rabbit
lapin à la Lorraine	rabbit in mushroom and cream sauce
lapin à la moutarde	rabbit in mustard sauce
lapin aux pruneaux	rabbit with prunes
lapin de garenne	wild rabbit
lard	bacon
léger	light
légume	vegetable
lentilles	lentils
lièvre	hare
limande	flounder, lemon sole
limonade	lemonade
livarot	strong, soft cheese from the north of France
longe	loin
lotte	turbot (fish)
loup au fenouil	bass with fennel
macédoine de légumes	mixed vegetables
mache	corn salad (leafy vegetable)
mangue	mango
maquereau au vin blanc	mackerel in white wine sauce
marc	grape brandy
marcassin	young wild boar
marchand de vin	in red wine sauce
marron	chestnut
massepain	marzipan
menthe	peppermint
menthe à l'eau	mint cordial
menu du jour	today's menu
menu gastronomique	gourmet menu
menu touristique	tourist menu
merlan au vin blanc	whiting in white wine

millefeuille	custard slice
millésime	vintage
morille	morel (mushroom)
morue	cod
mouclade	mussels in creamy sauce with saffron, turmeric, and white wine
moules marinière	mussels in white wine
mousse au chocolat	chocolate mousse
mousse au jambon	light ham mousse
mousseux	sparkling
moutarde	mustard
mouton	mutton
mulet	mullet
munster	strong cheese
mûre	blackberry
Muscadet	dry white wine from Nantes
myrtille	bilberry
nature	plain
navarin	mutton stew with vegetables
navet	turnip
noisette	hazelnut
noisette d'agneau	small, round lamb steak
noix	walnut
nouilles	noodles
œuf à la coque	boiled egg
œuf dur	hard-boiled egg
œuf en gelée	egg in aspic
œuf mollet	soft-boiled egg
œuf poché	poached egg
œufs à la neige	floating islands (poached egg whites on top of custard)
œufs brouillés	scrambled eggs
œuf sur le plat	fried egg
oie	goose
oignon	onion
omelette au fromage	cheese omelette
omelette au jambon	ham omelette
omelette au naturel	plain omelette
omelette aux champignons	mushroom omelette
omelette aux fines herbes	omelette with herbs
omelette au foie de volaille	omelette with chicken liver

omelette paysanne	omelette with potatoes and bacon
orange givrée	orange sorbet served in an orange
orange pressée	fresh orange juice
oseille	sorrel
oursin	sea urchin
pain	bread
pain au chocolat	chocolate puff pastry
palette de porc	shoulder of pork
palourde	clam
pamplemousse	grapefruit
panade	bread soup
parfait glacé	type of ice cream
pastis	anise-flavored alcoholic drink
pâté de canard	duck pâté
pâté de foie de volaille	chicken liver pâté
pâte feuilletée	puff pastry
pâtes	pasta
paupiettes de veau	slices of veal, rolled up and stuffed
pêche	peach
pêche Melba	peach melba
perdreau	young partridge
perdrix	partridge
petit déjeuner	breakfast
petite friture	whitebait
petit pain	roll
petit pois	peas
petits fours	small fancy pastries
petit suisse	light, white cream cheese
pied de porc	pig's feet
pigeonneau	young pigeon
pignatelle	small cheese fritter
pilaf de mouton	rice dish with mutton
pintade	guinea fowl
piperade	Basque egg dish with tomatoes and peppers
pissaladière	Provençal dish similar to pizza
pissenlit	dandelion (leaves)
pistache	pistachio
plat du jour	dish of the day
plateau de fromages	cheese board
pochouse	fish casserole with white wine
poire	pear

poireau	leek
poire belle Hélène	pear in chocolate sauce
poisson	fish
poivre	pepper
poivron	red or green pepper
pomme	apple
pomme bonne femme	baked apple
pomme de terre	potato
pommes Dauphine	potato fritters
pommes de terre à l'anglaise	boiled potatoes
pommes de terre en robe de chambre/en robe des champs	baked potatoes
pommes de terre sautées	fried potatoes
pommes frites	french fries
pommes paille	finely cut french fries
pommes vapeur	steamed potatoes
porc	pork
porto	port
potage	soup
potage bilibi	fish and oyster soup
potage Crécy	carrot and rice soup
potage cressonnière	watercress soup
potage Esaü	lentil soup
potage parmentier	leek and potato soup
potage printanier	vegetable soup
potage Saint-Germain	split pea soup
potage velouté	creamy soup
pot-au-feu	beef and vegetable stew
potée	vegetable and meat stew
Pouilly-Fuissé	dry white wine from Burgundy
poularde	fattened chicken
poule au pot	chicken and vegetable stew
poule au riz	chicken with rice
poulet à l'estragon	chicken in tarragon sauce
poulet basquaise	chicken with **ratatouille**
poulet chasseur	chicken with mushrooms and white wine
poulet créole	chicken in white sauce with rice
poulet rôti	roasted chicken
praire	clam
premier cru	vintage wine
provençale	with tomatoes, garlic, and herbs

prune	plum
pruneau	prune
pudding	plum pudding
purée	mashed potatoes
purée de marrons	chestnut purée
purée de pommes de terre	mashed potatoes
quatre-quarts	rich cake, similar to Madeira cake
quenelle	meat or fish dumpling
queue de bœuf	oxtail
quiche lorraine	quiche with bacon
râble de chevreuil	saddle of venison
raclette	Swiss dish of melted cheese
radis	radish
ragoût	stew
raie	skate
raie au beurre noir	skate fried in butter
raifort	horseradish
raisin	grape
râpé	grated
rascasse	scorpion fish
ratatouille	dish of stewed peppers, zucchini, eggplant, and tomatoes
ravigote	dressing with herbs
reblochon	strong cheese from Savoie
reine-claude	greengage (plum)
rémoulade	mayonnaise dressing flavored with herbs, mustard, and capers
rigotte	small goat's cheese from Lyons
rillettes	potted pork or goose meat
ris de veau	veal sweetbread
rissole	meat pie
riz	rice
riz à l'impératrice	sweet rice dish
riz pilaf	spicy rice with meat or seafood
rognon	kidney
rognons au madère	kidneys in Madeira
roquefort	blue cheese
rôti	joint
rôti de porc	roast pork
rouget	mullet
rouille	sauce accompanying bouillabaisse

sabayon	zabaglione (whipped egg yolk in Marsala wine)
sablé	shortbread
saint-honoré	cream puff cake
saint-marcellin	goat's cheese
salade	salad, lettuce
salade composée	mixed salad
salade de tomates	tomato salad
salade niçoise	salad of olives, tomatoes, anchovies, tuna, hard-boiled eggs, peppers, lettuce, celery, and green beans
salade russe	salad of diced vegetables in mayonnaise
salade verte	green salad
salmis	game stew
salsifis	oyster plant, salsify
sandwich au jambon	ham sandwich
sandwich au saucisson	salami sandwich
sanglier	wild boar
sauce aurore	white sauce with tomato purée
sauce aux câpres	white sauce with capers
sauce béarnaise	thick sauce with eggs and butter
sauce blanche	white sauce
sauce gribiche	dressing with hard-boiled eggs
sauce hollandaise	rich sauce made with eggs, butter, and vinegar, served with fish
sauce Madère	Madeira sauce
sauce matelote	wine sauce
sauce Mornay	**béchamel** sauce with cheese
sauce mousseline	hollandaise sauce with cream
sauce poulette	sauce made with mushrooms and egg yolks
sauce ravigote	dressing with shallots and herbs
sauce rémoulade	mayonnaise dressing flavored with herbs, mustard, and capers
sauce suprême	creamy sauce
sauce tartare	mayonnaise with herbs and gherkins
sauce veloutée	white sauce with egg yolks and cream
sauce vinot	wine sauce
saucisse	sausage
saucisse de Francfort	frankfurter
saucisse de Strasbourg	beef sausage
saucisson	salami-type sausage

saumon	salmon
saumon fumé	smoked salmon
sauternes	sweet white wine
savarin	crown-shaped rum baba
sec	dry
seiche	cuttlefish
sel	salt
service (non) compris	service (not) included
service 12% inclus	12% service charge included
servir frais	serve cool
sirop	cordial
sole bonne femme	sole in white wine and mushrooms
sole meunière	sole dipped in flour and fried in butter
soufflé au chocolat	chocolate soufflé
soufflé au fromage	cheese soufflé
soufflé au Grand Marnier	soufflé with orange liqueur
soufflé au jambon	ham soufflé
soufflé aux épinards	spinach soufflé
soupe à l'ail	garlic soup
soupe à l'oignon	French onion soup
soupe à l'oseille	sorrel soup
soupe au pistou	thick vegetable soup with basil
soupe aux choux	cabbage soup
soupe aux moules	mussel soup
soupe aux poireaux et pommes de terre	leek and potato soup
soupe aux tomates	tomato soup
soupe de poisson	fish soup
steak au poivre	peppered steak
steak frites	steak and french fries
steak haché	ground meat, ground beef
steak tartare	raw ground beef with a raw egg
sucre	sugar
suprême de volaille	chicken in cream sauce
tanche	tench (fish)
tarte	tart, pie
tarte aux fraises	strawberry tart
tarte aux pommes	apple tart
tarte frangipane	almond cream tart
tartelette	small tart
tarte Tatin	baked apple dish

tartine	slice of bread and butter
tendrons de veau	breast of veal
terrine	pâté
terrine du chef	chef's special pâté
tête de veau	calf's head
thé	tea
thé à la menthe	mint tea
thé au lait	tea with milk
thé citron	lemon tea
thon	tunafish
tilleul	lime tea
tomate	tomato
tomates farcies	stuffed tomatoes
tome de Savoie	white cheese from Savoy
tournedos	round beef steak
tourte	covered pie
tourteau	type of crab
tripes	tripe
tripes à la mode de Caen	tripe in spicy vegetable sauce
truite au bleu	poached trout
truite aux amandes	trout fried in butter with almonds
truite meunière	trout dipped in flour and fried in butter
vacherin	strong, soft cheese from the Jura
vacherin glacé	ice cream meringue
veau	veal
velouté de tomate	cream of tomato soup
vermicelle	vermicelli (very fine pasta used in soups)
verveine	verbena tea
viande	meat
vin	wine
vinaigrette	French dressing
vin blanc	white wine
vin de pays	local wine
vin de table	table wine
vin rosé	rosé wine
vin rouge	red wine
volaille	poultry
VSOP	mature brandy
waterzooi de poulet	chicken with vegetables
yaourt	yogurt

STORES AND SERVICES

This chapter covers all sorts of shopping needs and services. To start with you'll find some general phrases that can be used in lots of different places. Many of these are listed below. After the general phrases are some more specific requests and sentences to use when you've found what you need, be it food, clothing, repairs, film-developing, a haircut, or bargaining in the market. Don't forget to refer to the mini-dictionary for items you may be looking for.

Food stores in France are generally open from 8:30 AM to 7:30 PM, Tuesday to Saturday. Most large department stores are open until 9 or 10 PM. Bakeries are usually open on Sunday mornings. Other stores are open from 9 or 10 AM to 6:30 or 7 PM. On most Saturdays there's an open-air market in the town square or main street. Here you can buy food, clothes, china, etc., at bargain prices. In the cities, stores often don't take a break for lunch, and you may see the sign **journée continue** (open all day). In small towns and villages, stores will often be closed for two hours at lunchtime.

USEFUL WORDS AND PHRASES

antiques store	un magasin d'antiquités	*magaz<u>a</u>n d<u>o</u>nteekeetay*
audio equipment	radio-hifi	*rahdee-oh ee-fee*
bakery	une boulangerie	*bool<u>o</u>njree*
bookstore	une librairie	*leebrairee*
butcher's	une boucherie	*booshree*
buy	acheter	*ashtay*
camera store	le photographe	*fohtohgraf*
camping equipment	l'équipement de camping	*aykeepm<u>o</u>n duh k<u>o</u>npeeng*
candy store	la confiserie	*k<u>o</u>nfeesree*
cash register	la caisse	*kess*
china	de la porcelaine	*porslen*

confectioner's	la confiserie	*konfeesree*
cost *(verb)*	coûter	*kootay*
craft store	une boutique d'artisanat	*booteek darteezana*
department store	un grand magasin	*gron magazan*
dry cleaner's	le pressing	*"pressing"*
electrical goods store	un magasin d'appareils électriques	*magazan dapparay aylektreek*
fish market	une poissonnerie	*pwassonree*
florist's	le fleuriste	*flureest*
food store	un magasin d'alimentation	*magazan dall-eemontass-ion*
gift store	un magasin de cadeaux	*magazan duh kaddoh*
grocer's	une épicerie	*aypeessree*
hair salon	le coiffeur	*kwaffur*
hardware store	une quincaillerie	*kanki-ree*
indoor market	un marché couvert	*marshay koovair*
jeweler's	une bijouterie	*beejootree*
large department store	un hypermarché	*eepairmarshay*
Laundromat	la laverie automatique	*lavree ohtohmateek*
market	un marché	*marshay*
menswear	des vêtements hommes	*vetmon omm*
newsstand	le tabac-journaux	*tabba joornoh*
optician's	l'opticien	*opteess-ian*
pastry shop	une pâtisserie	*patteessree*
photography store	le photographe	*fohtohgraf*
receipt	un reçu	*ruhsoo*
record store	un disquaire	*deeskair*
sale	les soldes	*solld*
shoe repairer's	le cordonnier	*kordonn-yay*
shoe store	un magasin de chaussure	*magazan duh shoh-ssoor*
shopping bag	la poche en plastique	*posh on plasteek*

souvenir store	souvenirs-cadeaux	*soovuhneer kaddoh*
sports equipment	l'équipement sportif	*aykeepmon sporteef*
sportswear	des articles de sport	*arteek-l duh spor*
stationery store	une papeterie	*pappetree*
store	un magasin	*magazan*
supermarket	un supermarché	*soopairmarshay*
tailor	le tailleur	*ti-ur*
(for repairs)	la retoucheuse	*ruhtooshuhz*
tobacco shop	le bureau de tabac	*booroh duh tabah*
toy store	un magasin de jouets	*magazan duh joo-ay*
travel agent's	une agence de voyages	*ajonss duh vwi-aj*
wine seller	un marchand de vins	*marshon duh van*
women's wear	des vêtements femmes	*vetmon fam*

Excuse me, where is/are …?
Pardon, pouvez-vous me dire où se trouve …?
pardon poovay voo muh deer oo suh troov

Where is there a …? *(store)*
Où est-ce qu'il y a un/une …?
oo esskeel-ya an/oon

Where is the … department?
Où se trouve le rayon …?
oo suh troov luh rayon

Where is the main shopping area?
Où se trouve le principal quartier commerçant?
oo suh troov luh pranseepal katt-yay kommairson

Is there a market here?
Est-ce qu'il y a un marché ici?
esskeel-ya an marshay ee-see

I'd like …
Je voudrais …
juh voodreh

Do you have …?
Avez-vous …?
avay voo

How much is this?
Ça coûte combien?
sa koot konbyan

Where do I pay?
Où faut-il payer?
oo foh-teel pay-ay

Do you take credit cards?
Acceptez-vous les cartes de crédit?
ak-septay voo lay kart duh kraydee

I think perhaps you've short-changed me
Je crois que vous m'avez rendu trop peu
juh krwah kuh voo mavay rondoo troh puh

May I have a receipt?
Puis-je avoir un reçu?
pweej avwahr an ruhsoo

May I have a bag, please?
Puis-je avoir une poche plastique, s'il vous plaît?
pweej avwahr an poche plasteek seel voo pleh

I'm just looking
J'aimerais juste regarder
jemmereh joost ruhgarday

I'll come back later
Je reviendrai plus tard
juh ruhvee-andray ploo tar

Do you have any more of these?
En avez-vous d'autres?
on avay voo doht-r

Do you have anything less expensive?
Avez-vous quelque chose de moins cher?
avay voo kellkuh shohz duh mw<u>a</u>n shair

Do you have anything larger/smaller?
Avez-vous quelque chose de plus grand/petit?
avay voo kellkuh shohz duh pl<u>oo</u> gr<u>on</u>/puhtee

May I try it (them) on?
Est-ce que je peux l'essayer (les essayer)?
esskuh juh puh lessay-yay (layz essay-yay)

Does it come in other colors?
L'avez-vous dans d'autres coloris?
lavay voo d<u>on</u> doht-r koloree

Could you gift wrap it for me?
Pouvez-vous me faire un emballage-cadeau?
poovay voo muh fair <u>an</u> <u>on</u>ballaj kaddoh

I'd like to exchange this. It's damaged
J'aimerais échanger cet article. Il a un défaut
jemmereh aysh<u>on</u>jay set arteek-l. eel ah <u>an</u> dayfoh

I'm afraid I don't have the receipt
Je regrette mais je n'ai pas le reçu
juh ruhgret may juh nay pa luh ruhs<u>oo</u>

Can I have a refund?
Pouvez-vous me rembourser?
poovay voo muh r<u>on</u>boorsay

My camera isn't working
Mon appareil photo ne marche pas
m<u>on</u> appah-ray fohtoh nuh marsh pa

I want a roll of 36-exposure color film, 100 ISO
Je voudrais un film couleur de 36 poses, 100 ISO
juh voodreh <u>an</u> feelm koolur duh tr<u>on</u>t see poze s<u>on</u> ee-ess-oh

I'd like this film developed
J'aimerais faire développer ce film
jemmereh fair dayvuhloppay suh feelm

Matte/glossy prints
Epreuves mates/glacées
aypruhv mat/glassay

I'd like one-hour service, please
J'aimerais avoir les épreuves dans une heure, s'il vous plaît
jemmereh avwahr layz aypruhv don<u>z</u> <u>oo</u>n ur seel voo pleh

Where can I get this repaired? *(shoes/clothes)*
Où est-ce que je peux faire réparer/raccommoder ceci?
oo esskuh juh puh fair rayparay/rakomoday suhsee

Can you repair this? *(shoes/clothes)*
Pouvez-vous réparer/raccommoder ceci?
poovay voo rayparay/rakomoday suhsee

I'd like this skirt/these pants dry-cleaned
J'aimerais faire nettoyer à sec cette jupe/ce pantalon
jemmereh fair nettwah-yay ah sek set <u>joop</u>/suh <u>pontalon</u>

When will it/they be ready?
Quand est-ce que ce sera prêt?
<u>kon</u> esskuh suh suhra preh

I'd like some change for the washing machine/dryer
Je voudrais de la monnaie pour la machine à laver/le séchoir
juh voodreh duh la monneh poor la masheen ah lavay/luh sayshwahr

How does the machine work?
Comment cette machine fonctionne-t-elle?
komm<u>on</u> set masheen f<u>on</u>kss-ion tel

I'd like to make an appointment
Je voudrais prendre rendez-vous
juh voodreh pr<u>on</u>dr r<u>on</u>dayvoo

I'd like a cut and blow-dry
Je voudrais une coupe et un brushing
juh voodreh <u>oo</u>n koop ay <u>an</u> brusheeng

With conditioner
Avec démêlant
avek daymel<u>on</u>

No conditioner, thanks
Sans démêlant, merci
s<u>on</u> daymel<u>on</u> mairsee

Just a trim, please
Je voudrais les faire égaliser
juh voodreh lay fair aygaleezay

A bit more off here, please
Un petit peu plus court ici
<u>an</u> puhtee puh pl<u>oo</u> koort ee-see

Not too much off!
N'en coupez pas trop!
n<u>on</u> koopay pa troh

When does the market open?
Quand est-ce que le marché commence?
k<u>on</u> esskuh luh marshay komm<u>on</u>ss

Is there one today in a town nearby?
Est-ce qu'il y en a un aujourd'hui dans une ville avoisinante?
esskeel yona <u>an</u> ohjoordwee d<u>on</u>z <u>oo</u>n veel avwahzeen<u>on</u>t

What's the price per kilo?
Combien ça coûte au kilo?
k<u>on</u>by<u>an</u> sa koot oh keeloh

Could you write that down?
Pouvez-vous me l'écrire?
poovay voo muh laykreer

That's too much! I'll pay …
C'est beaucoup trop! Je donne …
seh bohkoo troh! juh don

That's fine. I'll take it
C'est bien. Je le prends
seh by<u>a</u>n. juh luh pr<u>on</u>

I'll have a piece of that cheese
Je prendrai un morceau de ce fromage
juh pr<u>on</u>dray <u>an</u> morsoh duh suh fromaj

About 250/500 grams
Environ 250/500 grammes
<u>on</u>veer<u>on</u> duh s<u>on</u> s<u>an</u>kont/s<u>an</u>k s<u>on</u> gram

A kilo/half a kilo of apples, please
Un kilo/demi-kilo de pommes, s'il vous plaît
<u>an</u> keeloh/duhmee keeloh duh pom seel voo pleh

A quarter of a kilo of salami, please
Une demi-livre de salami, s'il vous plaît
<u>oo</u>n duhmee leevr duh salamee seel voo pleh

May I taste it?
Puis-je goûter?
pwee<u>j</u> gootay

No, I don't like it
Non, je n'aime pas
n<u>on</u> juh nem pa

That's very nice. I'll take some
C'est très bon. J'en prendrai
seh treh bon. <u>jon</u> pr<u>on</u>dray

It isn't what I wanted
Ce n'est pas ce que je voulais
suh neh pa suh kuh juh vooleh

THINGS YOU'LL SEE

agence de voyages	travel agency
alimentation	grocer's
bon marché	inexpensive
boucherie	butcher's
boulangerie	bakery
bricolage	do-it-yourself supplies
cabines d'essayage	fitting rooms
caddy obligatoire	please take a cart
caisse	cash register, cashier
centre commercial	shopping center
charcuterie	pork butcher's shop, delicatessen
chocolatier	chocolate store
coiffeur pour dames/hommes	women's/men's hairstylist
confiserie	candy store
cordonnier	shoe repairs
droguerie	toiletries and household goods shop
entrée libre	free admission
épicerie	grocer's
épicerie fine	delicatessen
étage inférieur/supérieur	lower/upper floor
fermé le …	closed on …
fermeture hebdomadaire le lundi	closed on Mondays
fleuriste	florist
fournitures de bureau	office supplies
fourreur	furrier
frais	fresh
fruits de mer	seafood
glacier	ice cream parlor
grand magasin	department store
jouets	toys

→

journaux	newspapers
journée continue	open all day
laverie automatique	Laundromat
légumes	vegetables
librairie	bookstore
libre-service	self-service
magasin de chaussures	shoe store
marchand de vin	wine seller
marché	market
mode	fashion
nous n'acceptons pas les chèques	checks not accepted
nous ne remboursons pas	we cannot give cash refunds
occasion	bargain, secondhand
ouvert	open
panier obligatoire	please take a basket
papeterie	stationery
parfumerie	perfume and cosmetics store
pâtisserie	pastry shop
payer à l'ordre de ...	payable to ...
photographe	camera store
poissonnerie	fish market
pressing	dry cleaner's
prière de ne pas toucher	please do not touch
primeurs	produce market
prix	price
prix réduit	reduced price
produits d'entretien	household cleaning materials
quincaillerie	hardware store
rabais	reduction
rayon	department
salon de coiffure	hair salon
soldes	sale
supermarché	supermarket
tabac	tobacco shop

⟶

talons minute	shoes heeled while you wait
teinturerie	dry cleaner's
vêtements enfants	children's wear
vêtements femmes	women's wear
vêtements hommes	menswear

THINGS YOU'LL HEAR

Est-ce qu'on s'occupe de vous?
Are you being served?

Vous désirez?
Can I help you?

Vous n'avez pas plus petit?
Do you have anything smaller? (money)

Je suis désolé, mais le stock est épuisé
I'm sorry, we're out of stock

C'est tout ce que nous avons
This is all we have

Et avec ça?
Will there be anything else?

Combien en voulez-vous?
How much would you like?

Voulez-vous l'essayer?
Would you like to try it (on)?

Articles ni repris ni échangés
Goods will not be exchanged

Avez vous de la monnaie?
Do you have any change?

SPORTS

There isn't a shortage of sports facilities in France, whether you want to play tennis, swim, or play or watch soccer, rugby, or any other team sport like volleyball, basketball, or handball. Between December and April, skiing is very popular in the Alps, which boast a great number of resorts, like those around Grenoble or Chamonix-Mont-Blanc. During the rest of the year the mountains are ideal for hiking, climbing, and mountain-biking. Windsurfing is also popular, on the inland lakes, the Mediterranean coast, and on the rougher Atlantic Ocean. As for golf, although it has taken off recently in France, it remains an exclusive sport.

There are many sports vacations available, including cycling, golfing, walking, and horseback riding. Information on these can be obtained from a travel agent.

Bicycling is also common in France. Bicycles can be rented from over 200 train stations—you rent a bicycle at one station and return it at another.

USEFUL WORDS AND PHRASES

athletics	l'athlétisme	*attlay-teez-m*
badminton	le badminton	*badmeenton*
ball (*large*)	un ballon	*ballon*
(*small*)	une balle	*bal*
beginners' slope	la piste pour débutants	*peest poor daybooton*
bicycle	une bicyclette, un vélo	*bee-seeklet, vayloh*
go bicycling	faire du vélo	*fair doo vayloh*
binding (*ski*)	la fixation de ski	*feexass-ion duh skee*
canoe	un canoë	*kano-ay*
canoeing	le canoë-kayac	*kano-ay ki-ak*
cross-country skiing	le ski de fond	*skee duh fon*

diving board	un plongeoir	*plonjwahr*
downhill skiing	le ski alpin	*skee alpan*
fish	pêcher	*peshay*
fishing	la pêche	*pesh*
fishing rod	une canne à pêche	*kan ah pesh*
flippers	des palmes	*pal-m*
game	une partie	*partee*
goggles	les lunettes	*loonet*
golf	le golf	*golf*
golf course	un terrain de golf	*terran duh golf*
gymnastics	la gymnastique	*jeemnasteek*
handball	le hand-ball	*ondbal*
hang gliding	le deltaplane	*deltaplan*
hunting	la chasse	*shass*
ice rink	une patinoire	*patteenwahr*
lift pass	un forfait pour remonte-pentes	*forfeh poor ruhmont pont*
mountain bike	le vélo tout terrain	*vayloh too tairran*
mountaineering	l'alpinisme	*alpeeneez-m*
oxygen bottles	les bouteilles d'oxygène	*bootay doxeejen*
parasailing	le parachute ascensionnel	*parashoot assonss-ionnell*
pedal boat	un pédalo	*paydalloh*
racket	la raquette	*rakket*
ride	faire de l'équitation	*faire duh layk-eetass-ion*
riding	l'équitation	*ayk-eetass-ion*
riding hat	la bombe	*bombe*
rock climbing	la varappe	*varrap*
saddle	la selle	*sell*
sail (*noun*)	la voile	*vwahl*
(*verb*)	faire de la voile	*fair duh la vwahl*
sailboard	une planche à voile	*plonsh ah vwahl*
sailing	la voile	*vwahl*
skate	faire du patin à glace	*fair doo pattan ah glass*

skates	des patins à glace	*pattan ah glass*
ski *(noun)*	le ski	*skee*
(verb)	faire du ski, skier	*fair doo skee, skee-ay*
ski boots	des chaussures de ski	*shoh-soor duh skee*
skiing	le ski	*skee*
ski lift	le remonte-pente,	*ruhmont pont,*
	le télésiège	*taylaysee-ej*
skin diving	la plongée	*plonjay soo mareen*
	sous-marine	
ski pass	un forfait-skieur	*forfeh skee-ur*
ski poles	les bâtons de ski	*baton duh skee*
ski tow	le téléski	*taylayskee*
ski trail	la piste	*peest*
ski wax	le fart	*far*
sled	une luge	*looj*
snorkel	un tuba	*tooba*
soccer ball	le football, le foot	*footbal, foot*
soccer match	un match de football	*match duh footbal*
sports center	le centre sportif	*sontr sporteef*
stadium	un stade	*stad*
surfboard	une planche de surf	*plonsh duh soorf*
swimming pool	une piscine	*peeseen*
team	une équipe	*aykeep*
tennis	le tennis	*tennees*
tennis court	un court de tennis	*koor duh tennees*
toboggan	le toboggan	*tobogon*
underwater	la pêche	*pesh soo mareen*
fishing	sous-marine	
volleyball	le volleyball, le volley	*vollibal, volli*
water-skiing	le ski nautique	*skee nohteek*
water-skis	des skis nautiques	*skee nohteek*
wet suit	une combinaison	*kombeenehzon*
	de plongée	*duh plonjay*
go windsurfing	faire de la planche	*fair duh la plansh*
	à voile	*ah vwahl*
yacht	un voilier	*vwahlee-ay*

Is there an indoor/outdoor pool here?
Est-ce qu'il y a une piscine couverte/en plein air ici?
esskeel-ya <u>oon</u> peeseen koovairt/<u>on</u> pl<u>an</u> air ee-see

Is it safe to swim here?
Est-ce qu'on peut nager ici sans danger?
essk<u>on</u> puh najay ee-see s<u>on</u> d<u>on</u>jay

Can I fish here?
Est-ce que la pêche est autorisée ici?
esskuh la pesh et otoreezay ee-see

Is there a golf course near here?
Est-ce qu'il y a un terrain de golf dans les environs?
esskeel-ya <u>an</u> terr<u>an</u> duh golf d<u>on</u> layz <u>on</u>veer<u>on</u>

Do I have to be a member?
Faut-il être membre?
foh-teel ettr m<u>on</u>br

Where can I rent …?
Où est-ce que je peux louer …?
oo esskuh juh puh loo-ay

I would like to rent a bike/some skis
Je voudrais louer une bicyclette/des skis
juh voodreh loo-ay <u>oon</u> bee-seeklet/day skee

How much does it cost per hour/day?
Quel est le prix pour une heure/journée?
kell eh luh pree poor <u>oon</u> ur/joornay

What are the snow conditions like today?
Quelles sont les conditions d'enneigement aujourd'hui?
kell s<u>on</u> lay kondiss-i<u>on</u> d<u>on</u>ehjm<u>on</u> ohjoordwee

When does the lift start?
Quand est-ce que le remonte-pente commence à fonctionner?
k<u>ont</u> esskuh luh ruhm<u>ont</u> p<u>ont</u> komm<u>on</u>ss ah f<u>on</u>kss-i<u>on</u>ay

I would like to take skiing lessons
Je voudrais prendre des leçons de ski
juh voodreh prondr day luhsson duh skee

I'd like to try cross-country skiing
Je voudrais essayer le ski de fond
juh voodreh essay-yay luh skee duh fon

Is it very steep?
Est-ce que la pente est très raide?
esskuh la pont eh treh red

Where are the beginners' slopes?
Où se trouvent les pistes pour débutants?
oo suh troov lay peest poor daybooton

How much is a daily/weekly lift pass?
Quel est le prix d'un forfait journalier/hebdomadaire
   pour remonte-pentes?
*kell eh luh pree dan forfay joornal-yay/ebdoma-dair
   poor ruhmont pont*

There's something wrong with this binding
Il y a un problème au niveau de cette fixation
eel-ya an problaim oh neevoh duh set feexass-ion

I haven't played this before
Je n'ai jamais pratiqué ce sport auparavant
juh nay jammeh prateekay suh sporr ohparavon

THINGS YOU'LL SEE

baignade interdite	no swimming
boules	bowling
chasse gardée	hunting preserve
conditions d'enneigement	snow conditions
conditions pour skier	skiing conditions
courant dangereux	dangerous current

→

course automobile	racetrack
équipements sportifs	sports facilities
équitation	horseback riding
gymnase	gymnasium
leçons de ski nautique	water-skiing lessons
location de bateaux/vélos	boat/bicycle rental
parachute ascensionnel	parascending
patinoire	ice rink
patins à glace	ice skates
pêche interdite	no fishing
pêche sous-marine	underwater fishing
pente	slope
pétanque	French bowling game
piscine	swimming pool
piste balisée	marked ski path
piste cyclable	bicycle path
piste de ski	ski track
piste pour débutants	beginners' slope
plage	beach
planche à voile	sailboard
plongée interdite	no diving
plongée sous-marine	skin diving
police du port	harbor police
propriété privé interdiction d'entrer	no trespassing
remonte-pente	ski lift; ski tow
risque d'avalanche	danger of avalanche
sentier balisé	marked footpath
stade	stadium
surveillant de plage	lifeguard
télésiège	ski lift
téléski	ski tow
terrain de football	soccer field
vent fort	strong wind

POST OFFICES AND BANKS

Bureaux des postes (post offices) are identified by the blue-on-yellow La Poste sign. La Poste used to be called the PTT, so road signs often still indicate PTT.

Opening hours are usually 8 AM to 7 PM on weekdays and 8 AM to 12 PM on Saturdays. Most post offices close for lunch. Stamps can also be bought in **tabac-journaux** and **bar-tabacs**. Mailboxes are yellow.

Most banks are open from 9 AM to 5:30 PM and are closed on Saturdays and at lunchtime. There are some variations: some banks open on Saturday morning instead and are closed on Mondays. Foreign currency and traveler's checks can also be exchanged at some of the larger tourist information centers and hotels, but these usually give less advantageous exchange rates. There are numerous exchange offices in the main tourist areas in Paris.

The French unit of currency is the common European currency, the **euro** (_ewroh_). One **euro** is divided into 100 **centimes** (_sonteem_), and the coins come in 1, 2, 5, 10, 20, and 50 **centimes**; 1 and 2 euros. Bills are available in 5, 10, 20, 50, 100, 200, and 500 **euros**.

Credit cards—**les cartes de crédit** (_kart duh kraydee_)—are widely used and accepted for payment in stores, hotels, and at gas stations. It is also possible to withdraw money from an ATM—**un distributeur automatique de billets**—using credit cards, although in most cases there will be a charge for this type of transaction.

USEFUL WORDS AND PHRASES

airmail	par avion	_par av-ion_
ATM	un distributeur automatique de billets	_deestreebootur ohto-mateek duh bee-yay_
bank	la banque	_bonk_

bill *(banknote)*	le billet de banque,	*bee-yay duh bonk,*
	la coupure	*koopoor*
cash	du liquide	*leekeed*
change	changer	*shonjay*
check	un chèque	*shek*
checkbook	un carnet de chèques	*karnay duh shek*
collection	la levée	*luhvay*
counter	le guichet	*geeshay*
credit card	la carte de crédit	*kart duh kraydee*
customs form	un formulaire de	*formoolair duh*
	douane	*doo-an*
delivery	la distribution	*dees-treebooss-ion*
deposit *(noun)*	un dépôt	*daypoh*
(verb)	déposer	*daypozay*
dollar	le dollar	*dohlar*
exchange rate	le taux de change	*toh duh shonj*
fax *(noun)*	un fax	*fax*
(verb: document)	faxer	*faxay*
fax machine	un fax	*fax*
form	un formulaire	*formoolair*
general delivery	la poste restante	*posst restont*
international	un mandat	*monda antairnas-*
money order	international	*sionahl*
letter	une lettre	*lettr*
letter carrier	le facteur	*faktur*
mail *(noun)*	la poste	*posst*
(verb)	poster	*posstay*
mailbox	la boîte postale	*bwat postal*
(at home)	la boîte à lettres	*bwat ah lettr*
main post office	la poste principale	*posst pransee-pal*
package	un paquet	*pakkay*
parcel	un colis	*kolee*
postage rates	les tarifs postaux	*tareef postoh*
postal order	un mandat postal	*monda postal*
postcard	une carte postale	*kart postal*
post office	le bureau de poste	*booroh duh posst*

registered letter	une lettre recommandée	*lettr ruh-kommonday*
stamp	un timbre	*tanbr*
surface mail	par voie de terre	*par vwah duh tair*
traveler's check	le chèque de voyage	*shek duh vwi-yaj*
withdraw	retirer	*ruhteeray*
withdrawal	un retrait	*ruhtreh*
zip code	le code postal	*kod postal*

How much is a letter/postcard to …?
Quel est le tarif pour une lettre/carte postale pour …?
kell eh luh tareef poor oon lettr/kart postal poor

I would like three 60-centime stamps
Je voudrais trois timbres à soixante centimes
juh voodreh trwah tanbr ah swassont sonteem

I want to register this letter
Je voudrais envoyer cette lettre en recommandé
juh voodreh onvwah-yay set lettr on ruh-kommonday

I want to send this parcel to …
Je voudrais envoyer ce colis en …
juh voodreh onvwah-yay suh kolee on

How long does the mail to the … take?
Combien de temps mettent les lettres pour …?
konbyan duh ton met lay lettr poor

Where can I mail this?
Où est-ce que je peux poster ceci?
oo esskuh juh puh postay suhsee

Is there any mail for me?
Est-ce qu'il y a du courrier pour moi?
esskeel-ya doo kooree-ay poor mwah

I'd like to send a fax
Je voudrais envoyer un fax
juh voodreh onvwah-yay an fax

This is to go airmail
Cela doit être expédié par avion
suhla dwaht ettr expaydie-ay par av-ion

I'd like to change this into euros
J'aimerais changer ceci en euros
jemmereh shonjay suhsee on ewroh

I'd like that in 20 euro bills
Je voudrais cela en billets de 20 euros
juh voodreh suhla on bee-yay duh van ewroh

Can I cash these traveler's checks?
Est-ce que je peux encaisser ces chèques de voyage?
esskuh juh puh onkehssay say shek duh vwi-yaj

What is the exchange rate for the dollar?
Quel est le taux de change du dolar?
kell eh luh toh duh shonj duh dohlar

Can I draw cash using this credit card?
Est-ce que je peux retirer de l'argent avec cette carte de crédit?
esskuh juh puh ruhteeray duh larjon avek set kart duh kraydee

Could you give me smaller bills?
Pourriez-vous me donner des coupures plus petites?
pooree-ay voo muh donnay day koopoor ploo puhteet

THINGS YOU'LL SEE

accusé de réception	acknowledgment of receipt
affranchissement	postage
à l'étranger	abroad
autres destinations	other destinations
banque	bank
boîte à lettres	mailbox (domestic)
bureau de poste	post office
bureau le plus proche ...	nearest post office ...

→

caissier	cashier
carnet de timbres	book of stamps
change	exchange
change de devises	currency exchange
colis	parcel
courrier recommandé	registered mail
destinataire	addressee
devises étrangères	foreign currency
distributeur automatique de billets	ATM
expéditeur	sender
frais	charges
guichet	counter
heures des levées	collection times
heures d'ouverture	opening hours
imprimé	printed matter
localité	place
mandat postal	postal order
ne pas affranchir	postage paid
paquet	package
par avion	airmail
point argent	ATM
postes	mail
prochaine levée	next collection
renseignements	inquiries
tarifs postaux	postage rates
tarifs postaux intérieurs	domestic postage
tarifs postaux pour l'étranger	overseas postage
taux de change	exchange rate
timbre	stamp
transactions avec l'étranger	overseas business
ville	town

COMMUNICATIONS

Telephones: Telephone booths are square, stainless steel kiosks. Most of them take phonecards, and there are very few coin-operated phones. Phonecards can be bought at a post office, **tabac-journaux**, or **bar-tabac**. Many French people use mobile phones and will be contactable by email.

Telephone numbers have ten digits and are read out in pairs of numbers; i.e. 01 45 82 64 32 is said "**zéro un, quarante-cinq, quatre-vingt-deux, soixante-quatre, trente-deux**."

For directory inquiries dial 12 and for the operator 13.

USEFUL WORDS AND PHRASES

answering machine	le répondeur	_ray_pondur
call (*noun*)	une communication	komm<u>oo</u>neekass-i<u>on</u>
(*verb*)	appeler	applay
cardphone	le téléphone à carte	taylayfon ah kart
code	l'indicatif	<u>an</u>deekateef
collect call	une communication	komm<u>oo</u>neekass-i<u>on</u>
	en PCV	<u>on</u> pay say vay
dial	composer un numéro	kompozay <u>an</u>
		n<u>oo</u>mayroh
dial tone	la tonalité	tonaleetay
email address	l'adresse électronique	adrays aylayktroneek
emergency	l'urgence	<u>oor</u>jonss
extension	le poste, l'extension	posst, ext<u>on</u>ss-i<u>on</u>
fax machine	le fax	fax
internet	l'internet	internet
inquiries	les renseignements	r<u>on</u>sen-yuhm<u>on</u>
international	international	<u>an</u>tairnass-ionahl
mobile phone	le téléphone portable	taylayfon portabul
number	le numéro	n<u>oo</u>mayroh
operator	l'opérateur	opayratur
(*female*)	l'opératrice	opay-ratreess
phonecard	la télécarte	taylaykart
receiver	le combiné	k<u>on</u>beenay

102

telephone	le téléphone	*taylayfon*
telephone booth	une cabine	*kabeen*
website	le site web	*site web*
wrong number	un faux numéro	*foh n<u>oo</u>mayroh*

Where is the nearest phone booth?
Où se trouve la cabine téléphonique la plus proche?
oo suh troov la kabeen taylay-foneek la pl<u>oo</u> prosh

Is there a phone book?
Est-ce qu'il y a un annuaire?
esskeel-ya <u>an</u> ann<u>oo</u>-air

I would like to make a collect call
Je voudrais téléphoner en PCV
juh voodreh taylayfonay <u>on</u> pay say vay

I would like a number in …
Je voudrais un numéro à …
juh voodreh <u>an</u> n<u>oo</u>mayroh ah

Can you give me an outside line?
Pouvez-vous me donner une ligne extérieure?
poovay voo muh donnay <u>oo</u>n leen-yuh extayree-ur

How do I get an outside line?
Comment est-ce que je peux obtenir une ligne extérieure?
komm<u>on</u> esskuh juh puh obtuhneer <u>oo</u>n leen-yuh extayree-ur

Hello, this is … speaking
Allô! … à l'appareil
allo! … ah lapparay

Is that …?
C'est …?
seh

Speaking (said by a man/woman)
Lui-même/elle-même
lwee mem/el mem

I would like to speak to …
Je voudrais parler à …
juh voodreh parlay ah

Extension …, please
Le poste …, s'il vous plaît
luh posst … seel voo pleh

Please tell him/her … called
Pouvez-vous lui dire que … a téléphoné?
poovay voo lwee deer kuh … ah taylayfonay

Ask him/her to call me back, please
Pouvez-vous lui demander de me rappeler?
poovay voo lwee duhmonday duh muh rapplay

My number is …
Mon numéro est …
mon noomayroh eh

Do you know where he/she is?
Savez-vous où je peux le/la contacter?
savay voo oo juh puh luh/la kontaktay

When will he/she be back?
Savez-vous quand il/elle sera de retour?
savay voo kont eel/el suhra duh ruhtoor

Could you leave him/her a message?
Pouvez-vous lui laisser un message?
poovay voo lwee lessay an muhssaj

I'll call back later
Je rappellerai plus tard
juh rappelray ploo tar

Sorry, I've got the wrong number
Excusez-moi, je me suis trompé de numéro
exkoozay mwah juh muh swee tronpay duh noomayroh

What's your fax number/email address?
Quel est votre numéro de fax/adresse électronique?
kaylay votr noomayro duh faks/adrays aylayktroneek

Did you get my fax/email?
Avez-vous reçu mon fax/message électronique?
avayvoo ruhsoo mon faks/maysahj aylayktroneek

Please resend your fax
Veuillez ré-envoyer votre fax
vuhiay rayonvwahiay votr faks

Can I send an email/fax from here?
Puis-je envoyer un message électronique/fax d'ici?
pooeej ronvwahiay an maysahj aylayktroneek /faks deesee?

Can I use the photocopier/fax machine?
Puis-je utiliser la photocopieuse/le fax?
pooeej uhteeleezay la fotokop-iuhz/luh faks

THE ALPHABET

a	*ah*	h	*ash*	o	*o*	v	*vay*
b	*bay*	i	*ee*	p	*pay*	w	*doobluhvay*
c	*say*	j	*jee*	q	*koo*	x	*eeks*
d	*day*	k	*ka*	r	*air*	y	*ee-grek*
e	*uh*	l	*el*	s	*ess*	z	*zed*
f	*ef*	m	*em*	t	*tay*		
g	*jay*	n	*en*	u	*oo*		

THINGS YOU'LL SEE

annuaire	telephone directory
bottin	telephone directory
cabine téléphonique	telephone booth
communication interurbaine	long-distance call

→

105

communication urbaine	local call
composez	dial
crédit … unités	… units remaining/in credit
décrochez	lift the receiver
en dérangement	out of order
fermez le volet svp	close the flap
frais	charges
indicatif	code
introduire carte ou composer numéro libre	insert card or dial a free call
numéro direct	direct dialing
numéro vert	free call
pièce	coin
raccrochez svp	hang up the receiver
réclamations	complaint department
renseignements	directory inquiries
renseignements internationaux	international directory inquiries
retirez votre carte	remove your card
télécarte	phonecard
téléphone à carte	cardphone
unité	unit
veuillez patienter	please wait

THINGS YOU'LL HEAR

A quel numéro pouvons-nous vous joindre?
At what number can we contact you?

A qui désirez-vous parler?
Who would you like to speak to?

Vous avez un faux numéro
You've got the wrong number

Qui est à l'appareil?
Who's speaking?

→

C'est de la part de qui?
May I ask who's calling?

Lui-même/elle-même
Speaking (formal)

J'écoute
Speaking (informal)

La ligne est encombrée
The line is busy

Ne quittez pas
Hold the line

Ne raccrochez pas
Hold the line

Pourriez-vous rappeler plus tard?
Could you call back later?

Quel numéro demandez-vous?
Which number do you want?

Quel est votre numéro?
What is your number?

Désolé, il/elle n'est pas là
Sorry, he/she is not in

Il/elle sera de retour à six heures
He/she will be back at 6 PM

Pouvez-vous rappeler demain?
Please call again tomorrow

Le numéro que vous avez demandé n'est pas en service actuellement. Nous regrettons de ne pouvoir donner suite à votre appel
The number you have dialed is not in use. We're sorry we cannot put your call through

EMERGENCIES

Information on local health services can be obtained from tourist information offices, but in an emergency dial 18 for an ambulance or the fire department. Dial 17 for the police. If your car should break down, there are phones at intervals along highways and main roads.

USEFUL WORDS AND PHRASES

accident	un accident	*ak-seedon*
ambulance	une ambulance	*onboolonss*
assault	attaquer	*attakay*
breakdown	une panne	*pan*
break down *(verb)*	tomber en panne	*tonbay on pan*
breakdown recovery	le dépannage	*daypannaj*
burglar	un cambrioleur	*konbri-olur*
burglary	un cambriolage	*konbri-olaj*
emergency room	le service des urgences	*sairveess dayz oorjonss*
crash	un accident	*ak-seedon*
emergency	l'urgence	*oorjonss*
fire	le feu	*fuh*
fire department	les pompiers	*ponp-yay*
flood	une inondation	*eenondass-ion*
injured	blessé	*blessay*
lose	perdre	*pairdr*
pickpocket	le pickpocket	*"pickpocket"*
police	la police	*poleess*
police station	le poste de police	*posst duh poleess*
steal	voler	*volay*
theft	un vol	*vol*
thief	le voleur	*volur*
tow	remorquer	*ruhmorkay*

Help!
A l'aide!
ah led

Look out!
Attention!
attonss-ion

Stop!
Arrêtez!
arretay

This is an emergency!
C'est une urgence!
set oon oorjonss

Get an ambulance!
Appelez une ambulance!
applay oon onboolonss

Hurry up!
Faites vite!
fet veet

Please send an ambulance to …
Veuillez envoyer une ambulance à …
vuh-yay onvwah-yay oon onboolonss ah

Please come to …
Veuillez venir à …
vuh-yay vuhneer ah

My address is …
Mon adresse est …
mon adress eh

We've had a break-in
Nous avons été cambriolés
nooz avon aytay konbri-olay

There's a fire at …
Il y a le feu à …
eelya luh fuh ah

Someone's been injured/knocked down
Quelqu'un a été blessé/renversé
kellkan ah aytay blessay/ronvairsay

He's passed out
Il a perdu connaissance
eel ah pairdoo konnessonss

My passport/car has been stolen
On a volé mon passeport/ma voiture
on ah volay mon passpor/ma vwahtoor

I've lost my traveler's checks
J'ai perdu mes chèques de voyage
jay pairdoo may shek duh vwi-aj

I want to report a stolen credit card
Je veux signaler le vol d'une carte de crédit
juh vuh seen-yallay luh vol doon kart duh kraydee

It was stolen from my room
On l'a volée dans ma chambre
on la volay don ma shonbr

I lost it in the park/on the train
Je l'ai perdue dans le parc/dans le train
juh lay pairdoo don luh park/don luh tran

My luggage is missing
On a égaré mes bagages
on ah aygaray may bagaj

Has my luggage turned up yet?
A-t-on retrouvé mes bagages?
atton ruhtroovay may bagaj

The registration number is …
La plaque d'immatriculation est …
la plak deematreek<u>oo</u>lass-i<u>on</u> eh

I've had a crash
J'ai eu un accident
jay <u>oo</u> <u>an</u> ak-seed<u>on</u>

My car's been broken into
On a fracturé ma voiture
<u>on</u> ah frakt<u>oo</u>ray ma vwaht<u>oo</u>r

I've been mugged
On m'a agressé
<u>on</u> ma agressay

My son's missing
Mon fils a disparu
m<u>on</u> feess ah deespar<u>oo</u>

He has fair/brown hair
Il a les cheveux blonds/bruns
eel ah lay shuhvuh bl<u>on</u>/br<u>an</u>

He's … years old
Il a … ans
eel ah … <u>on</u>

I've locked myself out
Je me suis enfermé dehors
juh muh sweez <u>on</u>fairmay duh-or

He's drowning
Il se noie
eel suh nwah

She can't swim
Elle ne sait pas nager
el nuh seh pa najay

Things You'll See

composez ...	dial ...
feu	fire
hôpital	hospital
pharmacie de garde	pharmacy on duty
police de la route	traffic police
poste de police	police station
premiers secours	first aid
secours de montagne	mountain rescue
service des urgences	emergency room
service non-stop	24-hour service
surveillant	lifeguard
urgences	emergencies

Things You'll Hear

Quelle est votre adresse?
What's your address?

Où êtes-vous?
Where are you?

Pouvez-vous le/la décrire?
Can you describe it/him/her?

Quel âge a-t-il/elle?
How old is he/she?

Quand est-ce arrivé?
When did it happen?

HEALTH

A pharmacy is called a **pharmacie**. At night and on Sundays there is **la pharmacie de garde** (pharmacy on duty). You can find its address in the local newspaper, in the window of any pharmacy, or through the local **commissariat de police**. If you have a prescription from your doctor at home, it will have to be rewritten by a French doctor. If you have not brought the medication you need from the States, a French pharmacist can always recommend a substitute.

USEFUL WORDS AND PHRASES

accident	un accident	*ak-seedon*
ambulance	une ambulance	*onboolonss*
anemic	anémique	*annaymeek*
appendicitis	une appendicite	*appondee-seet*
appendix	l'appendice	*appondeess*
aspirin	de l'aspirine	*aspeereen*
asthma	l'asthme	*ass-m*
backache	le mal de dos	*mal duh doh*
bandage	un pansement	*ponssmon*
bite (*by dog*)	une morsure	*morsoor*
(*by insect*)	une piqûre	*peekoor*
bladder	la vessie	*vessee*
blister	une ampoule	*onpool*
blood	du sang	*son*
blood donor	un donneur de sang	*donnur duh son*
burn	une brûlure	*brooloor*
cancer	le cancer	*konsair*
chest	la poitrine	*pwattreen*
chicken pox	la varicelle	*varree-sel*
cold	un rhume	*room*
concussion	une commotion cérébrale	*kommoss-ion sayraybral*
constipation	la constipation	*konstee-pass-ion*

contact lenses	des lentilles de contact	_lo_ntee duh _ko_ntakt
corn	un cor	kor
cough	la toux	too
cut	une coupure	koo_poor_
dentist	le dentiste	_do_nteest
diabetes	le diabète	dee-abet
diarrhea	la diarrhée	dee-array
dizzy	le vertige	vairtee_j_
doctor	le docteur	doktur
(female)	la doctoresse	doktoress
earache	le mal d'oreille	mal doray
fever	la fièvre	fee-evr
filling	un plombage	_plo_nba_j_
first aid	premiers soins	pruhm-yay sw_an_
flu	la grippe	greep
fracture	une fracture	frakt_oo_r
German measles	la rubéole	_roo_bay-ol
glasses	des lunettes	_loo_-net
hay fever	le rhume des foins	_roo_m day fw_an_
headache	le mal de tête	mal duh tet
heart	le cœur	kur
heart attack	une crise cardiaque	kreez kardee-ak
hemorrhage	une hémorragie	aymorrajee
hospital	l'hôpital	opeetahl
indigestion	une indigestion	_a_ndeejest-i_on_
injection	une piqûre	peek_oo_r
itch	des démangeaisons	daym_o_n_jezo_n
kidney	le rein	r_an_
lump	une grosseur	grossur
measles	la rougeole	roojol
migraine	la migraine	meegren
motion sickness	le mal des transports	mal day tr_o_nspor
mumps	les oreillons	oray-y_on_
nausea	la nausée	nozay

nurse	l'infirmier	_an_feerm-yay
(*female*)	l'infirmière	_an_feermee-air
operation	une opération	opayrass-i_on_
optician	un opticien	optees-y_an_
pain	une douleur	doolur
penicillin	la pénicilline	paynee-seeleen
pharmacy	la pharmacie	farmassee
plaster of Paris	le plâtre	platr
pneumonia	une pneumonie	p-nuhmonee
pregnant	enceinte	_onsant_
prescription	une ordonnance	ordonn_on_ss
rheumatism	des rhumatismes	r_oo_mattees-m
scald	une brûlure	br_ooloo_r
scratch	une égratignure	aygratteen-y_oo_r
sick	malade	malad
smallpox	la variole	varree-ol
sore throat	le mal de gorge	mal duh gorj
splinter	une écharde	ayshard
sprain	une entorse	_on_torss
sting	une piqûre	peek_oo_r
stomach	l'estomac	estoma
temperature	la température	_ton_payrat_oo_r
tonsils	les amygdales	ammeedal
toothache	le mal de dents	mal duh d_on_
ulcer	un ulcère	_oo_l-sair
vaccination	un vaccin	vakks_an_
vomit	vomir	vomeer
whooping cough	la coqueluche	kokl_oo_sh

I have a pain in …
J'ai mal au/à la …
jay mal oh/ah la

I do not feel well
Je ne me sens pas bien
*juh nuh muh s_on_ pa by_an_*

I feel faint
Je vais m'évanouir
juh veh mayvanweer

I feel sick
J'ai envie de vomir
jay onvee duh vomeer

I feel dizzy
J'ai la tête qui tourne
jay la tet kee toorn

It hurts here
J'ai mal ici
jay mal ee-see

It's a sharp/dull pain
C'est une douleur aiguë/sourde
set oon doolur ay-goo/soord

It hurts all the time
La douleur est constante
la doolur eh konstont

It only hurts now and then
C'est douloureux de temps en temps
seh doolooruh duh ton zon ton

It hurts when you touch it
C'est douloureux au toucher
seh doolooruh oh tooshay

It hurts more at night
C'est douloureux surtout la nuit
seh doolooruh soortoo la nwee

It stings/aches
Ça pique/fait mal
sa peek/feh mal

I have a temperature
J'ai de la fièvre
jay duh la fee-evr

I'm ... months pregnant
Je suis enceinte de ...mois
juh sooee onsant duh ...mwah

I need a prescription for ...
J'ai besoin d'une ordonnance pour ...
jay buhzwan doon ordonnonss poor

I normally take ...
Je prends habituellement ...
juh pron abeetoo-elmon

I'm allergic to ...
Je suis allergique à ...
juh sweez allerjeek ah

Have you got anything for ...?
Avez-vous quelque chose contre ...?
avay voo kellkuh shohz kontr

Do I need a prescription for ...?
Me faut-il une ordonnance pour ...?
muh foh-teel oon ordonnonss poor

Can you take these if you're pregnant/breastfeeding?
Peut-on prendre cela quand on est enceinte/allaite?
puhton prondr suhla kanton ay onsant/alayt?

I have lost a filling
J'ai perdu un plombage
jay pairdoo an plonbaj

Will he/she be all right?
Va-t-il/elle se remettre?
vateel/el suh ruhmettr

Will he/she need an operation?
Est-ce qu'il/elle devra subir une opération?
essk eel/el duhvra soobeer oon opayrass-ion

How is he/she?
Comment va-t-il/elle?
kommon vateel/el

THINGS YOU'LL SEE

anesthésie générale	general anesthetic
anesthésie locale	local anesthetic
cabinet dentaire	dentist's office
cabinet médical	doctor's office
dermatologue	dermatologist
généraliste	General Practitioner
gynécologue	gynecologist
hôpital	hospital
infirmerie	infirmary
médecin	doctor
oculiste	eye specialist
ophtalmologue	ophthalmologist
oto-rhino-laryngologiste	ear, nose, and throat specialist
pédiatre	pediatrician
pharmacie	pharmacy
pharmacie de garde	pharmacy on duty
pharmacie de service	pharmacy on duty
premiers soins	first aid
salle d'attente	waiting room
service	ward
service d'urgence	emergency room
S.O.S Médecin	24-hour emergency medical service found in large towns

THINGS YOU'LL HEAR

Prendre ... comprimés à la fois
Take ... pills/tablets at a time

Prendre ... comprimés ... fois par jour
Take ... pills/tablets ... times a day

Avec de l'eau
With water

Mâchez-les
Chew them

A prendre au coucher
To be taken at bedtime

Le matin à jeun
First thing in the morning on an empty stomach

Une/deux/trois fois par jour
Once/twice/three times a day

Au coucher seulement
Only when you go to bed

Que prenez-vous habituellement?
What do you normally take?

Je pense que vous devriez voir un docteur
I think you should see a doctor

Je regrette, nous n'avons pas cela
I'm sorry, we don't have that

Il vous faut une ordonnance pour ça
For that you need a prescription

On ne trouve pas cela ici
You cannot get that here

CONVERSION TABLES

DISTANCES

A mile is 1.6km. To convert kilometers to miles, divide the km by 8 and multiply by 5. Convert miles to km by dividing the miles by 5 and multiplying by 8.

miles	0.62	1.24	1.86	2.43	3.11	3.73	4.35	6.21
miles *or* **km**	1	2	3	4	5	6	7	10
km	1.61	3.22	4.83	6.44	8.05	9.66	11.27	16.10

WEIGHTS

The kilogram is equivalent to 2 lb 3oz. To convert kg to lbs, divide by 5 and multiply by 11. One ounce is about 28 grams, and eight ounces about 227 grams; 1 lb is therefore about 454 grams.

lbs	2.20	4.41	6.61	8.82	11.02	13.23	19.84	22.04
lbs *or* **kg**	1	2	3	4	5	6	9	10
kg	0.45	0.91	1.36	1.81	2.27	2.72	4.08	4.53

TEMPERATURE

To convert Celsius degrees into Fahrenheit, the accurate method is to multiply the C° figure by 1.8 and add 32. Similarly, to convert F° to C°, subtract 32 from the F° figure and divide by 1.8.

C°	-10	0	5	10	20	30	36.9	40	100
F°	14	32	41	50	68	86	98.4	104	212

LIQUIDS

A liter is about 2.1 pints; a gallon is roughly 3.8 liters.

gals	0.27	0.53	1.33	2.65	5.31	7.96	13.26
gals *or* **liters**	1	2	5	10	20	30	50
liters	3.77	7.54	18.85	37.70	75.40	113.10	188.50

TIRE PRESSURES

lb/sq in	18	20	22	24	26	28	30	33
kg/sq cm	1.3	1.4	1.5	1.7	1.8	2.0	2.1	2.3

MINI-DICTIONARY

The feminine of most adjectives is formed by adding "e" to the masculine form given in this dictionary and consequently pronouncing the final consonant (e.g. **petit** *puhtee*, **petite** *puhteet*). Irregular feminine forms are indicated after the abbreviation (*fem*).

a un/une (*see p 5*)
about: about 16 environ seize
accelerator l'accélérateur
accident l'accident
accommodation l'hébergement
ache la douleur
adaptor (*plug*) la prise multiple
   (*voltage*) l'adaptateur
address l'adresse
adhesive l'adhésif
admission charge prix d'entree
aftershave l'après-rasage
again de nouveau
against contre
agent l'agent
AIDS SIDA
air l'air
air conditioning la climatisation
aircraft l'avion
airline la compagnie aérienne
airport l'aéroport
airport bus la navette (pour l'aéroport)
alarm clock le réveil
alcohol l'alcool
Algeria l'Algérie
Algerian algérien
   (*man*) un Algérien
   (*woman*) une Algérienne
all tout
   all the streets toutes les rues
   that's all c'est tout
almost presque

alone seul
Alps les Alpes
already déjà
always toujours
am: I am je suis
ambulance l'ambulance
America l'Amérique
American américain
   (*man*) un Américain
   (*woman*) une Américaine
and et
Andorra Andorre
ankle la cheville
another (*different*) un/une autre
   another coffee, please
   encore un café, s'il vous plaît
answering machine le réponder
antifreeze l'antigel
antiques shop le magasin d'antiquités
antiseptic l'antiseptique
apartment l'appartement
aperitif l'apéritif
appetite l'appétit
apple la pomme
application form le formulaire de demande
appointment le rendez-vous
apricot l'abricot
are: you are vous êtes
   (*singular, familiar*) tu es
   we are nous sommes
   they are ils/elles sont

arm le bras
arrival l'arrivée
arrive arriver
art l'art
art gallery le musée d'art
artist l'artiste
as: as soon as possible dès que possible
ashtray le cendrier
asleep endormi
   he's asleep il dort
aspirin l'aspirine
at: at the post office à la poste
   at the café au café
   at 3 o'clock à 3 heures
ATM un distributeur automatique
   de billets
attractive attirant
aunt la tante
Australia l'Australie
Australian australien
   (man) un Australien
   (woman) une Australienne
automatic automatique
away: is it far away? est-ce que
   c'est loin?
   go away! allez-vous en!
awful affreux
ax la hache
axle l'essieu

baby le bébé
baby carriage le landau
baby wipes lingettes
back *(not front)* l'arrière
   (body) le dos
   I'll come back tomorrow
   je reviendrai demain
backpack le sac à dos
bacon le bacon
   bacon and eggs
   des œufs au bacon
bad mauvais

baggage claim la réclamation de bagages
bait l'appât
bake cuire
bakery la boulangerie
balcony le balcon
ball *(football, etc.)* le ballon
   (tennis, etc.) la balle
ballpoint pen le stylo-bille
banana la banane
band *(musicians)* le groupe
bandage le pansement
bank la banque
bar le bar
   bar of chocolate une tablette de
   chocolat
barbecue le barbecue
barber's le coiffeur
bargain une affaire
basement le sous-sol
basin *(sink)* le lavabo
basket le panier
bath le bain
   (tub) la baignoire
   to take a bath prendre un bain
bathroom la salle de bain
battery *(car)* la batterie
   (flashlight) la pile
beach la plage
beans les haricots
beard la barbe
beautiful beau, *(fem.)* belle
because parce que
bed le lit
bed linen les draps
bedroom la chambre
beef le bœuf
beer la bière
before avant
beginner le débutant
   (female) la débutante
beginners' slope la piste pour débutants
behind derrière
beige beige

Belgian belge
  (man) un Belge
  (woman) une Belge
Belgium la Belgique
bell *(church)* la cloche
  (door) la sonnette
below ... sous ...
belt la ceinture
beside à côté de
best: the best le meilleur
better mieux
between ... entre ...
bicycle la bicyclette, le vélo
big grand
bill l'addition
  money) le billet
bird l'oiseau
birthday l'anniversaire
  happy birthday! joyeux anniversaire!
biscuit le biscuit
bite *(noun: by dog)* la morsure
  (by snake, insect) la piqûre
  (verb: dog) mordre
  (insect, snake) piquer
bitter amer
black noir
blackberry la mûre
black currant le cassis
blanket la couverture
bleach *(noun)* l'eau de Javel®
  (verb) décolorer
blind *(cannot see)* aveugle
  (window) le store
blister l'ampoule
blizzard la tempête de neige
blond *(adj.)* blond
blood le sang
blouse le chemisier
blue bleu
boat le bateau
  (smaller) la barque
body le corps
boil *(verb)* bouillir

boiler le chauffe-eau
bolt *(noun: on door)* le verrou
  (verb) verrouiller
bone l'os
  (fish) l'arête
book *(noun)* le livre
  (verb) réserver
bookstore la librairie
boot la botte
border la frontière
boring ennuyeux
born: I was born in ... je suis né en ...
both les deux
  both of them tous les deux
  both of us nous deux
  both ... and ... ... et ... à la fois
bottle la bouteille
bottle opener le décapsuleur,
  l'ouvre-bouteille
bottom le fond
  (part of body) le derrière
bowl le bol
box la boîte
box office *(theater, etc.)* le bureau de
  location
boy le garçon
boyfriend le petit ami
bra le soutien-gorge
bracelet le bracelet
brake *(noun)* le frein
  (verb) freiner
brandy le cognac
bread le pain
breakdown *(car)* la panne
  (nervous) la dépression
  I've had a breakdown *(car)* je suis
  tombé en panne
breakfast le petit déjeuner
breathe respirer
bridge le pont
briefcase l'attaché-case
British britannique
Brittany la Bretagne

123

brochure la brochure
broiler le gril
broken cassé
  broken leg la jambe cassée
brooch la broche
brother le frère
brown marron
bruise le bleu
brush *(noun)* la brosse
  (paint) le pinceau
  (broom) le balai
  (verb) brosser
Brussels Bruxelles
bucket le seau
building le bâtiment
bumper le pare-chocs
burn *(noun)* la brûlure
  (verb) brûler
bus le bus
business les affaires
  it's none of your business
  cela ne vous regarde pas
bus station la gare routière
busy *(occupied)* occupé
  (street) animé
but mais
butcher's la boucherie
butter le beurre
button le bouton
buy acheter
by: by the window près de la fenêtre
  by Friday d'ici vendredi
  by myself tout seul
  written by ... écrit par ...

cabbage le chou
cabinet le placard
cable car le téléphérique
cable TV la télé cablée
café le café
cake le gâteau
calculator la calculette

call: what's it called? comment est-ce
  que ça s'appelle?
camcorder le caméscope
camera l'appareil-photo
campsite le terrain de camping
camshaft l'arbre à cames
can *(vessel)* la boîte de conserve
can *(able)* pouvoir
  can I have ...? puis-je avoir ...?
  can you ...? pouvez-vous ...?
can opener l'ouvre-boîte
Canada le Canada
Canadian canadien
  (man) un Canadien
  (woman) une Canadienne
canal le canal
candle la bougie
candy le bonbon
canoe le canoë
cap *(hat)* la casquette
  (bottle) la capsule
car la voiture
  (train) la voiture, le wagon
car seat *(for a baby)* le siège pour bébé
carburetor le carburateur
card la carte
cardigan le gilet
careful prudent
  careful! attention!
  be careful! soyez prudent!
caretaker le/la concierge
carpet le tapis
carrot la carotte
carry out: to carry out à emporter
case la valise
cash l'argent
  to pay cash payer en liquide
cassette la cassette
cassette player le lecteur de cassettes
castle le château
cat le chat
cathedral la cathédrale
cauliflower le chou-fleur

cave la grotte
cemetery le cimetière
central heating le chauffage central
center le centre
certificate le certificat
chair la chaise
change *(noun: money)* la monnaie
  (verb: money) changer
  (clothes) se changer
Channel la Manche
Channel Islands les îles Anglo-
  Normandes
Channel Tunnel
  le tunnel sous la Manche
check *(noun)* le chèque
checkbook le carnet de chèques
check-in l'enregistrement des bagages
check in faire enregistrer ses bagages
cheers! *(toast)* santé!
cheese le fromage
cherry la cerise
chess les échecs
chest la poitrine
chest of drawers la commode
chicken le poulet
child l'enfant
children les enfants
china la porcelaine
chocolate le chocolat
  a box of chocolates une boîte de
  chocolats
chop *(food)* la côtelette
  (verb: cut) couper
church l'église
cigar le cigare
cigarette la cigarette
cinema le cinéma
city la ville
city center le centre ville
class la classe
classical music la musique classique
clean propre
clear clair

clever intelligent
clock l'horloge
close *(near)* près
  (stuffy) étouffant
  (verb) fermer
closed fermé
clothes les vêtements
clubs *(cards)* trèfle
clutch l'embrayage
coat le manteau
coat hanger le cintre
cockroach le cafard
coffee le café
coin la pièce
cold *(illness)* le rhume
  (adj.) froid
collar le col
collection *(stamps, etc.)* la collection
  (postal) la levée
color la couleur
color film la pellicule couleur
comb *(noun)* le peigne
  (verb) peigner
come venir
  I come from … je viens de …
  we came last week
  nous sommes arrivés la semaine
  dernière
comforter la couette
compact disc le disque compact
compartment le compartiment
complicated compliqué
computer l'ordinateur
concert le concert
conditioner *(hair)* le baume après-
  shampooing
condom le préservatif
conductor *(bus)* le receveur
  (orchestra) le chef d'orchestre
congratulations! félicitations!
consulate le consulat
contact lenses les lentilles de contact
contraceptive le contraceptif

cook (*noun*) le cuisinier
  (*female*) la cuisinière
  (*verb*) faire la cuisine
cooking utensils les ustensiles de cuisine
cool frais, (*fem.*) fraîche
cork le bouchon
corkscrew le tire-bouchon
corner le coin
corridor le couloir
Corsica la Corse
Corsican corse
  (*man*) un Corse
  (*woman*) une Corse
cosmetics les produits de beauté
cost (*verb*) coûter
  what does it cost? combien ça coûte?
cotton le coton
cotton balls le coton hydrophile
cough (*noun*) la toux
  (*verb*) tousser
cough drops les pastilles pour la gorge
country (*state*) le pays
  (*not town*) la campagne
cousin le cousin
  (*female*) la cousine
crab le crabe
cramp la crampe
crayfish (*freshwater*) l'écrevisse
  (*saltwater*) la langoustine
cream la crème
credit card la carte de crédit
crowded bondé
cruise la croisière
crutches les béquilles
cry (*weep*) pleurer
  (*shout*) crier
cucumber le concombre
cuff links les boutons de manchette
cup la tasse
curlers les rouleaux
curls les boucles
current le courant
curry le curry

curtain le rideau
customs la douane
cut (*noun*) la coupure
  (*verb*) couper

dad papa
dance (*noun*) la danse
  (*verb*) danser
dangerous dangereux
dark foncé
  dark blue bleu foncé
daughter la fille
day le jour
dead mort
deaf sourd
dear cher
debit card la carte bancaire
deck of cards le jeu de cartes
deep profond
delay (*noun*) le retard
deliberately exprès
dentist le/la dentiste
dentures le dentier
deny nier
deodorant le déodorant
department store le grand magasin
departure le départ
develop développer
diamond (*jewel*) le diamant
diamonds (*cards*) carreau
diaper les couches à jeter
diary l'agenda
dictionary le dictionnaire
die mourir
diesel le diesel
different différent
  that's different c'est différent
  I'd like a different one
  j'en voudrais un autre
difficult difficile
dining room la salle à manger
disabled handicapé

dish cloth le torchon
dishwashing detergent le produit pour la vaisselle
disposable diapers les couches jetables
distributor (car) le delco
dive (verb) plonger
diving board le plongeoir
divorced divorcé
do faire
  how do you do? comment allez-vous?
dock le quai
doctor le docteur
  (female) la doctoresse
document le document
dog le chien
doll la poupée
dollar le dollar
door la porte
double room une chambre pour deux personnes
doughnut le beignet
down en bas
dress la robe
drink (noun) la boisson
  (verb) boire
  would you like a drink? voulez-vous boire quelque chose?
drinking water l'eau potable
drive (verb: car) conduire
driver le conducteur
  (female) la conductrice
driver's license le permis de conduire
driving regulations le code de la route
drugstore la pharmacie
drunk soûl, ivre
dry sec, (fem.) sèche
dry cleaner's le pressing
during pendant
dustcloth le chiffon à poussière
duty-free hors-taxe

each (every) chaque
  two euros each deux euros pièce
ear l'oreille
early tôt
earrings les boucles d'oreille
east l'est
easy facile
eat manger
egg l'œuf
either: either of them n'importe lequel
  either … or … soit … soit …
elastic élastique
elastic band l'élastique
elbows les coudes
electric électrique
electricity l'électricité
elevator l'ascenseur
else: something else autre chose
  someone else quelqu'un d'autre
  somewhere else ailleurs
email le message, la messagerie électronique
email address l'adresse électronique
embarrassing gênant
embassy l'ambassade
embroidery la broderie
emerald l'émeraude
emergency l'urgence
emergency stop cord le cordon d'alarme
emergency exit la sortie de secours
empty vide
end la fin
engaged (couple) fiancé
engine (car) le moteur
  (train) la locomotive
England l'Angleterre
English anglais
Englishman un Anglais
Englishwoman une Anglaise
enlargement l'agrandissement
enough assez
entertainment le divertissement
entrance l'entrée

envelope l'enveloppe
eraser la gomme
escalator l'escalier roulant
especially particulièrement
evening le soir
every chaque
everyone tout le monde
everything tout
everywhere partout
example l'exemple
  for example par exemple
excellent excellent
excess baggage
  l'excédent de bagages
exchange (verb) échanger
exchange rate le taux de change
excursion l'excursion
excuse me! pardon!
exit la sortie
expensive cher
extension cord la rallonge
eye l'œil
  eyes les yeux

face le visage
faint vague
  to faint evanouir
fair (noun) la foire
  (just) juste
  it's not fair ce n'est pas juste
fan (ventilator) le ventilateur
  (enthusiast) le/la fan
fan belt la courroie du ventilateur
fantastic fantastique
far loin
  how far is it to …?
  est-ce que … est loin d'ici?
fare le prix du billet
farm la ferme
farmer le fermier
fashion la mode
fast rapide

fat (of person) gros, (fem.) grosse
  (on meat, etc.) le gras
father le père
fax (noun) le fax
  (verb: document) faxer
fax machine le fax
feel (touch) toucher
  I feel hot j'ai chaud
  I feel like … j'ai envie de …
  I don't feel well je ne me sens pas bien
feet les pieds
felt-tip pen le feutre
ferry (small) le bac
  (large) le ferry
fever la fièvre
fiancé le fiancé
fiancée la fiancée
field le champ
fig la figue
filling (in tooth) le plombage
  (in sandwich, cake) la garniture
film le film
filter paper le papier filtre
finger le doigt
fire le feu
  (blaze) l'incendie
fire extinguisher l'extincteur
fireworks le feu d'artifice
first premier
first aid les premiers soins
first floor le premier étage
first name le prénom
fish le poisson
fishing la pêche
  to go fishing aller à la pêche
fishing rod la canne à pêche
fish market la poissonnerie
flag le drapeau
flash (camera) le flash
flashlight la lampe de poche
flat (level) plat
flavor le goût
flea la puce

flight le vol
flight attendant l'hôtesse de l'air
flip-flops les tongs
flippers les palmes
floor *(ground)* le plancher
  (story) l'étage
flour la farine
flower la fleur
flute la flûte
fly *(insect)* la mouche
  (verb: of plane, etc.) voler
  (of person) prendre l'avion
fog le brouillard
folk music la musique folklorique
food la nourriture
food poisoning l'intoxication alimentaire
foot le pied
for pour
  for me pour moi
  what for? pour quoi faire?
  for a week pour une semaine
foreigner l'étranger
  (female) l'étrangère
forest la forêt
forget oublier
fork la fourchette
fountain pen le stylo-plume
fourth quatrième
France la France
free *(no cost)* gratuit
  (at liberty) libre
freezer le congélateur
French français
  the French les Français
French fries les frites
Frenchman un Français
Frenchwoman une Française
friend l'ami
  (female) l'amie
friendly amical
fringe la frange
front: in front devant
frost le gel

fruit le fruit
fruit juice le jus de fruit
fry frire
frying pan la poêle
full complet
  I'm full! j'ai l'estomac bien rempli!
full board la pension complète
funny drôle
furniture les meubles

garage le garage
garbage les ordures
garbage can liner le sac poubelle
garden le jardin
garlic l'ail
gas l'essence
gas-permeable lenses les lentilles
  semi-souples
gas station la station-service
gate le portail, la grille
  (at airport) la porte
gay homosexuel
gear *(car)* la vitesse
gearshift le levier de vitesse
gel le gel
German allemand
  (man) un Allemand
  (woman) une Allemande
Germany l'Allemagne
get *(fetch)* aller chercher
  have you got …? avez-vous …?
  to get the train prendre le train
get back: we get back tomorrow nous
  rentrons demain
  to get something back récupérer
  quelque chose
get in entrer
  (arrive) arriver
get off *(bus, etc.)* descendre
get on *(bus, etc.)* monter
get out sortir
get up se lever

gift le cadeau
gin le gin
ginger le gingembre
girl *(child)* la fille
  (young woman) la jeune fille
girlfriend la petite amie
give donner
glad heureux
glass le verre
glasses les lunettes
glossy prints les épreuves sur papier
  glacé
gloves les gants
glue la colle
go aller
gold l'or
good bon, *(fem.)* bonne
  good! bien!
goodbye au revoir
government le gouvernement
granddaughter la petite-fille
grandfather le grand-père
grandmother la grand-mère
grandparents les grands-parents
grandson le petit-fils
grape(s) le raisin
grass l'herbe
gray gris
Great Britain la Grande-Bretagne
green vert
grocer's l'épicerie
ground cloth le tapis de sol
ground floor le rez-de-chaussée
guarantee *(noun)* la garantie
  (verb) garantir
guard *(train)* le chef de train
guide le/la guide
guide book le guide
guitar la guitare
gun *(rifle)* le fusil
  (pistol) le pistolet

hair les cheveux
haircut la coupe (de cheveux)
hair dryer le sèche-cheveux
hairspray la laque
hairstylist le coiffeur
  (female) la coiffeuse
half demi
  half an hour une demi-heure
half board la demi-pension
ham le jambon
hamburger le hamburger
hammer le marteau
hand la main
handbrake le frein à main
handkerchief le mouchoir
handle *(door)* la poignée
handsome beau
hangover la gueule de bois
happy heureux
harbor le port
hard dur
  (difficult) difficile
hard lenses les lentilles rigides
hardware store la quincaillerie
hat le chapeau
have avoir
  have you got ...? avez-vous ...?
hay fever le rhume des foins
he il
head la tête
headache le mal de tête
headlights les phares
hear entendre
hearing aid l'appareil acoustique
heart le cœur
hearts *(cards)* cœurs
heater le radiateur
heating le chauffage
heavy lourd
heel le talon
hello bonjour
help *(noun)* l'aide
  (verb) aider

hepatitis l'hépatite
her: it's for her c'est pour elle
  give it to her donnez-le lui
  her book son livre
  her house sa maison
  her shoes ses chaussures
  it's hers c'est à elle
hi salut
high haut
highway l'autoroute
hill la colline
him: it's for him c'est pour lui
  give it to him donnez-le lui
his: his book son livre
  his house sa maison
  his shoes ses chaussures
  it's his c'est à lui
history l'histoire
hitchhike faire de l'autostop
HIV positive séropositif(ve)
hobby le passe-temps
home: at home *(my home)* chez moi
  he's at home il est chez lui
homeopathy homéopathie
honest honnête
honey le miel
honeymoon la lune de miel
hood *(car)* le capot
horn *(car)* le klaxon
  (animal) la corne
horrible horrible
hospital l'hôpital
hot chaud
hour l'heure
house la maison
hovercraft l'aéroglisseur
hoverport l'hoverport
how? comment?
hungry: I'm hungry j'ai faim
hurry: I'm in a hurry je suis pressé
husband le mari
hydrofoil l'hydrofoil

I je
ice la glace
ice cream la glace
ice rink la patinoire
ice skates les patins à glace
ice-skating: to go ice-skating aller
  patiner
if si
ignition l'allumage
ill malade
immediately immédiatement
impossible impossible
in dans
  in France en France
indigestion l'indigestion
inexpensive bon marché, pas cher
infection l'infection
information l'information
injection la piqûre
injury la blessure
ink l'encre
inn l'auberge
inner tube la chambre à air
insect l'insecte
insect repellent la crème anti-insecte
insomnia l'insomnie
instant coffee le café soluble
insurance l'assurance
interesting intéressant
internet internet
interpret interpréter
interpreter l'interprète
invitation l'invitation
Ireland l'Irlande
Irish irlandais
  (man) un Irlandais
  (woman) une Irlandaise
iron *(metal)* le fer
  (for clothes) le fer à repasser
  (verb) repasser
is: he/she is il/elle est
  it is c'est
island l'île

it il; elle
Italian italien
   (*man*) un Italien
   (*woman*) une Italienne
Italy l'Italie
its son; sa; ses (*see his*)

jacket la veste
jam la confiture
jazz le jazz
jeans les jeans
jellyfish la méduse
jeweler's la bijouterie
job le travail
jog (*verb*) faire du jogging
   to go for a jog aller faire du jogging
jogging suit le survêtment
joke la plaisanterie
just: it's just arrived ça vient juste
   d'arriver
   I've just one left il ne m'en reste qu'un

kettle la bouilloire
key la clé
kidney le rein
kilo le kilo
kilometer le kilomètre
kitchen la cuisine
knee le genou
knife le couteau
knit tricoter
knitting needle l'aiguille à tricoter
know (*fact*) savoir
   (*person*) connaître
   I don't know je ne sais pas

label l'étiquette
lace la dentelle
   (*of shoe*) le lacet
lake le lac

lamb l'agneau
lamp la lampe
lampshade l'abat-jour
land (*noun*) la terre
   (*verb*) atterrir
language la langue
large grand
last (*final*) dernier
   last week la semaine dernière
   at last! enfin!
last name le nom de famille
late tard
   the bus is late
   le bus est en retard
later plus tard
laugh rire
Laundromat la laverie automatique
laundry (*place*) la blanchisserie
   (*clothes*) le linge
laundry detergent la lessive
laxative le laxatif
lazy paresseux
leaf la feuille
leaflet le dépliant
learn apprendre
leather le cuir
left (*not right*) la gauche
   there's nothing left
   il ne reste plus rien
leg la jambe
lemon le citron
lemonade la limonade
length la longueur
lens (*camera*) l'objectif
less moins
lesson la leçon
letter la lettre
letter carrier le facteur
lettuce la laitue
library la bibliothèque
license le permis
license plate la plaque d'immatriculation
life la vie

light la lumière
  (not heavy) léger
  (not dark) clair
light bulb l'ampoule
lighter le briquet
lighter fluid le gaz à briquet
light meter la cellule photoélectrique
like: I like you je vous aime bien
  I like swimming j'aime nager
  it's like … c'est comme …
lime *(fruit)* le citron vert
line *(noun)* la queue
  (verb) faire la queue
lipstick le rouge à lèvres
liqueur la liqueur
list la liste
liter le litre
litter les ordures
little *(small)* petit
  it's a little big c'est un peu trop grand
  just a little juste un peu
liver le foie
lobster le homard
lollipop la sucette
long long, *(fem.)* longue
lost property les objets trouvés
loud fort
  (color) criard
lounge le salon
lounge chair le transat
love *(noun)* l'amour
  (verb) aimer
lover l'amant
  (female) l'amante
low bas
luck la chance
  good luck! bonne chance!
luggage les bagages
luggage lockers la consigne automatique
luggage rack le porte-bagages
lunch le déjeuner
Luxembourg le Luxembourg

mad fou, *(fem.)* folle
magazine la revue
maid la femme de chambre
mail *(noun)* la poste
  (verb) poster
mailbox la boîte à lettres
make faire
makeup le maquillage
man l'homme
manager le directeur
many: not many pas beaucoup
map la carte
  (street map) le plan
margarine la margarine
market le marché
marmalade la marmelade d'oranges
married marié
mascara le mascara
mass *(church)* la messe
mast le mât
match *(light)* l'allumette
  (sport) le match
material *(cloth)* le tissu
matter: it doesn't matter ça ne fait rien
mattress le matelas
maybe peut-être
me: it's me c'est moi
  it's for me c'est pour moi
  give it to me donnez-le-moi
meal le repas
mean: what does this mean? qu'est-ce que cela veut dire?
meat la viande
mechanic le mécanicien
medicine le médicament
Mediterranean la Méditerranée
meeting la réunion
melon le melon
men *(bathroom)* les toilettes pour hommes
menu le menu
message le message
middle le milieu

midnight minuit
milk le lait
mine: it's mine c'est à moi
mineral water l'eau minérale
minute *(noun)* la minute
mirror le miroir
  (car) le rétroviseur
Miss Mademoiselle
mistake l'erreur
mobile phone le téléphone portable
modem le modem
money l'argent
month le mois
monument le monument
moon la lune
moped la mobylette®
more plus
  more or less plus ou moins
morning le matin
  in the morning dans la matinée
mosquito le moustique
mother la mère
motorboat le bateau à moteur
motorcycle la moto
mountain la montagne
mountain bike le vélo tout terrain
mouse la souris
mousse *(hair)* la mousse
mouth la bouche
move bouger
  (house) déménager
  don't move! ne bougez pas!
Mr. Monsieur
Mrs. Madame
mug la tasse
museum le musée
mushroom le champignon
music la musique
musical instrument l'instrument
  de musique
musician le musicien
mussels les moules
must: I must … je dois …

mustache la moustache
mustard la moutarde
my: my book mon livre
  my house ma maison
  my shoes mes chaussures

nail *(metal)* le clou
  (finger) l'ongle
nail clippers la pince à ongles
nailfile la lime à ongles
nail polish le vernis à ongles
name le nom
  what's your name comment vous
  appelez-vous?
narrow étroit
near: near the door près de la porte
  near Paris près de Paris
necessary nécessaire
neck le cou
necklace le collier
need *(verb)* avoir besoin de
  I need … j'ai besoin de …
  there's no need ce n'est pas nécessaire
needle l'aiguille
negative *(photo)* le négatif
neither: neither of them ni l'un ni
  l'autre
  neither … nor … ni … ni …
nephew le neveu
never jamais
new nouveau, *(fem.)* nouvelle
news les nouvelles
  (TV) les informations
newspaper le journal
newsstand le tabac-journaux
next prochain
  next week la semaine prochaine
  what next? et puis quoi?
nice *(place, etc.)* joli
  (person) sympathique
  (to eat) bon
niece la nièce

night la nuit
nightclub la boîte de nuit
nightgown la chemise de nuit
no *(response)* non
  (not any) aucun
nobody personne
noisy bruyant
none aucun
noon midday
north le nord
nose le nez
not pas
  he's not ... il n'est pas ...
notebook le carnet
nothing rien
novel le roman
now maintenant
nowhere nulle part
nudist le nudiste
number *(figure)* le numéro
  (amount) le nombre
nut *(fruit)* la noix
  (for bolt) l'écrou

oars les rames
occasionally
  de temps en temps
of de
office le bureau
often souvent
oil l'huile
ointment la pommade
OK d'accord
old vieux, *(fem.)* vieille
  how old are you?
  quel âge avez-vous?
olive l'olive
omelette l'omelette
on ... sur ...
one un/une
onion l'oignon
only seulement

open *(adj.)* ouvert
  (verb) ouvrir
operation l'opération
operator *(phone)* l'opérateur
  (female) l'opératrice
opposite en face
optician's l'opticien
or ou
orange *(fruit)* l'orange
  (color) orange
orange juice le jus d'orange
orchestra l'orchestre
ordinary habituel
organ *(music)* l'orgue
other: the other ... l'autre ...
our: our house notre maison
  our children nos enfants
  it's ours c'est à nous
out: he's out il n'est pas là
outside dehors
oven le four
over *(above)* au-dessus de
  (more than) plus de
  (finished) fini
  it's over the road
  c'est de l'autre côté de la rue
  over there là-bas
oyster l'huître

package le paquet
  (parcel) le colis
packet le paquet
padlock un cadenas
page la page
pain la douleur
paint *(noun)* la peinture
pair la paire
pajamas le pyjama
palace le palais
pale pâle, blême
pancake la crêpe
pants le pantalon

pantyhose le collant
paper le papier
   (newspaper) le journal
paraffin le pétrole
parcel le colis
pardon? pardon?
parents les parents
park (noun) le jardin public
   (verb) garer
parsley le persil
part (in hair) la raie
party (celebration) une fête
   (group) le groupe
   (political) le parti
pass (in a car) doubler
passenger le passager
passport le passeport
passport control le contrôle des
   passeports
pasta les pâtes
pastry store la pâtisserie
path le chemin
pay payer
peach la pêche
peanuts les cacahuètes
pear la poire
pearl la perle
peas les petits pois
pedestrian le piéton
pen le stylo
pencil le crayon
pencil sharpener le taille-crayon
pen pal le correspondant
   (female) la correspondante
people les gens
pepper (& salt) le poivre
   (red/green) le poivron
peppermints les bonbons à la menthe
per: per night par nuit
perfect parfait
perfume le parfum
perhaps peut-être
perm la permanente

phone book l'annuaire
phonecard la carte téléphonique
photocopier la photocopieuse
photograph (noun) la photo
   (verb) photographier
photographer le/la photographe
phrase book un guide de conversation
piano le piano
pickpocket le pickpocket
picnic le pique-nique
piece le morceau
pill le comprimé
pillow l'oreiller
pilot le pilote
pin l'épingle
   (clothes) la pince à linge
pineapple l'ananas
pink rose
pipe (for smoking) la pipe
   (for water) le tuyau
piston le piston
pizza la pizza
place l'endroit
  at your place chez vous
plant la plante
plastic le plastique
plastic bag le poche en plastique
plastic wrap le film alimentaire
   transparent
plate l'assiette
platform le quai
play (noun: theater) la pièce
   (verb) jouer
please s'il vous plaît
plug (electrical) la prise
   (sink) le bouchon
pocket la poche
pocketbook le sac à main
pocketknife le canif
poison le poison
police la police
police officer le policier
police station le commissariat

politics la politique
poor pauvre
   (*bad quality*) mauvais
pop music la musique pop
pork le porc
port (*harbor*) le port
   (*drink*) le porto
porter le porteur
possible possible
postcard la carte postale
poster (*outside*) l'affiche
   (*inside*) le poster
post office la poste
potato la pomme de terre
potato chips les chips
poultry la volaille
pound (*weight*) la livre
powder la poudre
prefer préférer
prescription l'ordonnance
pretty (*beautiful*) joli
   (*quite*) plutôt
priest le prêtre
private privé
problem le problème
public le public
pull tirer
puncture la crevaison
purple violet
purse le porte-monnaie
push pousser
put mettre
Pyrenees les Pyrénées

quality la qualité
quarter le quart
question la question
quick rapide
quiet silencieux
quite (*fairly*) assez
   (*fully*) très

radiator le radiateur
radio la radio
radish le radis
rail: by rail par chemin de fer
railroad le chemin de fer
rain la pluie
rain boots les boîtes en caoutchouc
raincoat l'imperméable
raisin le raisin sec
rare (*uncommon*) rare
   (*steak*) bleu
raspberry la framboise
rat le rat
razor blades les lames de rasoir
read lire
reading lamp la lampe de bureau
   (*bedside*) la lampe de chevet
ready prêt
receipt le reçu
receptionist le/la receptionniste
record (*music*) le disque
   (*sports etc.*) le record
record player le tourne-disque
record store le disquaire
red rouge
   (*hair*) roux
refreshments les rafraîchissements
refrigerator le frigo
registered letter la lettre recommandée
relax se détendre
religion la religion
remember: I remember je m'en souviens
   I don't remember je ne me souviens pas
rent (*verb*) louer
reservation la réservation
rest (*remainder*) le reste
   (*verb: relax*) se reposer
restaurant le restaurant
restaurant car le wagon-restaurant
return (*come back*) revenir
   (*give back*) rendre
rice le riz
rich riche

right (*correct*) juste
  (*not left*) la droite
ring (*wedding, etc.*) la bague
ripe mûr
river la rivière
  (*big*) le fleuve
road la route
  (*in town*) la rue
rock (*stone*) le rocher
  (*music*) le rock
roll (*bread*) le petit pain
roof le toit
room la chambre
  (*space*) la place
rope la corde
rose la rose
round (*circular*) rond
  it's my round
  c'est ma tournée
round-trip ticket l'aller retour
row (*verb*) ramer
rowboat la barque
rubber (*material*) le caoutchouc
rug (*mat*) la carpette
  (*blanket*) la couverture
ruins les ruines
ruler la règle
rum le rhum
run (*verb*) courir
runway la piste

sad triste
safe (*not in danger*) en sécurité
  (*not dangerous*) sans danger
safety pin l'épingle de nourrice
sailboat le voilier
salad la salade
sale la vente
  (*at reduced prices*) les soldes
salmon le saumon
salt le sel
same: the same … le/la même …

same: the same again, please
  la même chose, s'il vous plaît
sand le sable
sandals les sandales
sand dunes les dunes
sandwich le sandwich
sanitary napkins les serviettes
  hygiéniques
sauce la sauce
saucepan la casserole
sauna le sauna
sausage la saucisse
say dire
  what did you say? qu'avez-vous dit?
  how do you say …?
  comment dit-on …?
scampi les langoustines
scarf l'écharpe
  (*head*) le foulard
school l'école
scissors les ciseaux
Scotland l'Ecosse
screw la vis
screwdriver le tournevis
sea la mer
seafood les fruits de mer
seat la place
seat belt la ceinture de sécurité
second (*of time*) la seconde
  (*in series*) deuxième
see voir
  I can't see je ne vois rien
  I see je vois
sell vendre
separate (*adj.*) séparé
  (*verb*) séparer
serious sérieux
several plusieurs
sew coudre
shampoo le shampooing
shave: to shave se raser
shaving cream la mousse à raser
shawl le châle

she elle
sheet le drap
shell la coquille
shellfish les crustacés
ship le bateau
shirt la chemise
shoelaces les lacets
shoe polish le cirage
shoes les chaussures
shop le magasin
shopping les courses
  to go shopping faire les courses
short court
shorts le short
shoulder l'épaule
shower *(bath)* la douche
  (rain) l'averse
shower gel le gel douche
shrimp la crevette
shutter *(camera)* l'obturateur
  (window) le volet
sick: I feel sick j'ai envie de vomir
  to be sick *(vomit)* vomir
side *(edge)* le bord
sidelights les feux de position
sidewalk le trottoir
sights: the sights of … les vues de …
silk la soie
silver *(color)* argenté
  (metal) l'argent
simple simple
sing chanter
single *(one)* seul
  (unmarried) célibataire
single room la chambre pour
  une personne
sister la sœur
skates les patins à glace
ski *(noun)* le ski
  (verb) skier
ski boots les chaussures de ski
skid *(verb)* déraper
skiing: to go skiing faire du ski

ski lift le remonte-pente
skin cleanser le démaquillant
ski pole le bâton de ski
ski resort la station de ski
skirt la jupe
sky le ciel
sled la luge
sleep *(noun)* le sommeil
  (verb) dormir
sleeper le wagon-lit
sleeping bag le sac de couchage
sleeping pill le somnifère
slip le jupon
slippers les pantoufles
slow lent
small petit
smell *(noun)* l'odeur
  (verb) sentir
smile *(noun)* le sourire
  (verb) sourire
smoke *(noun)* la fumée
  (verb) fumer
snack le snack
sneakers les tennis
snow la neige
so si
soaking solution *(for contact lenses)*
  la solution de trempage
soap le savon
soccer le football
socks les chaussettes
soda water l'eau gazeuse
soft lenses les lentilles souples
somebody quelqu'un
somehow d'une façon ou d'une autre
something quelque chose
sometimes quelquefois
somewhere quelque part
son le fils
song la chanson
sorry! *(apology)* pardon!
  sorry? *(pardon?)* pardon?
  I'm sorry je suis désolé

soup la soupe
south le sud
souvenir le souvenir
spade (*shovel*) la pelle
spades (*cards*) pique
Spain l'Espagne
Spanish espagnol
spare parts les pièces de rechange
spark plug la bougie
speak parler
   do you speak …? parlez-vous …?
   I don't speak … je ne parle pas …
speed la vitesse
speed limit la limitation de vitesse
spider l'araignée
spinach les épinards
spoon la cuillère
sports arena le centre sportif
spring (*mechanical*) le ressort
   (*season*) le printemps
square (*noun: in town*) la place
   (*adj.: shape*) carré
stadium le stade
staircase l'escalier
stairs les escaliers
stamp le timbre
stapler l'agrafeuse
star l'étoile
   (*movie*) la vedette
start (*noun: beginning*) le début
   (*verb*) commencer
station la gare
   (*subway*) la station
statue la statue
steak le steak
steal voler
   it's been stolen on l'a volé
steamer le bateau à vapeur
   (*cooking*) le couscoussier
steering wheel le volant
sting (*noun*) la piqûre
   (*verb*) piquer
stockings les bas

stomach l'estomac
stomachache le mal de ventre
stop (*noun: bus*) l'arrêt (de bus)
   (*verb*) s'arrêter
   stop! stop!
storm la tempête
stove la cuisinière
strawberry la fraise
stream (*small river*) le ruisseau
street la rue
street musician le musicien des rues
string (*cord*) la ficelle
   (*guitar, etc.*) la corde
stroller la poussette
strong (*person, drink*) fort
   (*material*) résistant
student l'étudiant
   (*female*) l'étudiante
stupid stupide
suburbs la banlieue
subway le métro
sugar le sucre
suit (*noun*) le costume
   it suits you ça vous va bien
suitcase la valise
sun le soleil
sunbathe se faire bronzer
sunburn le coup de soleil
sunglasses les lunettes de soleil
sunny ensoleillé
sunshade le parasol
suntan le bronzage
suntan lotion la lotion solaire
supermarket le supermarché
supper le souper
supplement le supplément
sure sûr
suspenders les bretelles
sweat (*noun*) la transpiration
   (*verb*) transpirer
sweater le pull
sweatshirt le sweat-shirt
sweet (*not sour*) sucré

swim *(verb)* nager
swimming: to go swimming
  aller se baigner
swimsuit le maillot de bain
swimming pool la piscine
swim trunks le maillot de bain
Swiss suisse
  (man) le Suisse
  (woman) la Suissesse
switch l'interrupteur
Switzerland la Suisse
synagogue la synagogue

table la table
taillights les feux arrière
take prendre
takeoff *(noun)* le décollage
talcum powder le talc
talk *(noun)* la conversation
  (verb) parler
tall grand
tampon le tampon
tangerine la mandarine
tap le robinet
tapestry la tapisserie
tea le thé
teacher *(secondary)* le professeur
telephone *(noun)* le téléphone
  (verb) téléphoner
telephone booth
  la cabine téléphonique
television la télévision
temperature la température
tent la tente
tent pole le montant de tente
tent stake le piquet de tente
than que
thank *(verb)* remercier
  thank you merci
  thanks merci
that *(that one)* ça
  that bus ce bus

that: that man cet homme
  that woman cette femme
  what's that? qu'est-ce que c'est?
  I think that the …
  je pense que le …
the le/la; *(plural)* les *(see p 5)*
their: their room leur chambre
  their books leurs livres
  it's theirs c'est à eux
them: it's them ce sont eux/elles
  it's for them c'est pour eux/elles
  give it to them donnez-le-leur
then alors
  (after) ensuite
there là
  there is/are … il y a …
  is/are there …? y a-t-il …?
these: these things ces choses
  these are mine ils sont à moi
they ils; *(fem.)* elles
thick épais
thin mince
think penser
  I think so je pense que oui
  I'll think about it je vais y penser
third troisième
thirsty: I'm thirsty j'ai soif
this *(this one)* ceci
  this bus ce bus
  this man cet homme
  this woman cette femme
  what's this? qu'est-ce que c'est?
  this is Mr. … je vous présente M. …
those: those things ces choses-là
  those are his ils sont à lui
throat la gorge
through à travers
thumbtack la punaise
thunderstorm l'orage
ticket le billet
  (subway, bus) le ticket
ticket collector le contrôleur
ticket office le guichet

tide la marée
tie *(noun)* la cravate
  (verb) nouer
tight étroit
time l'heure
  what's the time?
  quelle heure est-il?
timetable *(train, bus)* l'horaire
tip *(money)* le pourboire
  (end) le bout
tire *(on wheel)* le pneu
tired fatigué
tissues mouchoirs
to: to America en Amérique
  to Paris à Paris
  to the station à la gare
  to the center au centre
  to the doctor chez le docteur
toast le pain grillé
tobacco le tabac
toboggan le toboggan
today aujourd'hui
together ensemble
toilet les toilettes
toilet paper le papier hygiénique
tomato la tomate
tomorrow demain
tongue la langue
tonic le tonic
tonight ce soir
too *(also)* aussi
  (excessively) trop
tooth la dent
toothache le mal de dents
toothbrush la brosse à dents
toothpaste le dentifrice
tour la visite
tourist le/la touriste
tourist office le syndicat d'initiative
towel la serviette
tower la tour
town la ville
town hall l'hôtel de ville

toy le jouet
track suit le survêtement
tractor le tracteur
tradition la tradition
traffic la circulation, le trafic
traffic lights les feux
trailer la caravane, la remorque
train le train
translate traduire
translator le traducteur
  (female) la traductrice
trash can la poubelle
travel agency l'agence de voyages
traveler's check le chèque de voyage
tray le plateau
tree l'arbre
trip le voyage
truck le camion
true vrai
try essayer
tunnel le tunnel
tweezers la pince à épiler
two weeks quinze jours
typewriter la machine à écrire

umbrella le parapluie
uncle l'oncle
under ... sous ...
underpants le slip
understand comprendre
  I understand je comprends
  I don't understand
  je ne comprends pas
underwear les sous-vêtements
university l'université
unleaded sans plomb
until jusqu'à
unusual inhabituel
up en haut
  (upward) vers le haut
  up there là-haut
urgent urgent

us: it's us c'est nous
  it's for us
  c'est pour nous
  give it to us
  donnez-le-nous
use *(verb)* utiliser
  it's no use
  ça ne sert à rien
useful utile
usual habituel
usually d'habitude

vacancy *(room)* la chambre à louer
vacation les vacances
vacuum cleaner l'aspirateur
valley la vallée
valve la soupape
vanilla la vanille
vase le vase
VCR le magnètoscope
veal le veau
vegetables les légumes
vegetarian *(adj.)* végétarien
vehicle le véhicule
very très
  very much beaucoup
video *(film/tape)* la vidéo
view la vue
viewfinder le viseur
villa la villa
village le village
vinegar le vinaigre
violin le violon
visit *(noun)* la visite
  (verb: place) visiter
  (person) rendre visite
visitor le visiteur
  (female) la visiteuse
vitamin pill le comprimé de vitamines
vodka la vodka
voice la voix

wait attendre
  wait! attendez!
waiter le serveur
  waiter! garçon!
waiting room la salle d'attente
waitress la serveuse
  waitress! Mademoiselle!
Wales le pays de Galles
walk *(verb)* marcher
  to go for a walk
  aller se promener
wall *(inside)* la paroi
  (outside) le mur
wallet le portefeuille
war la guerre
wardrobe l'armoire
warm chaud
was: I was j'étais
  he was il était
  she was elle était
  it was il/elle était
washer la rondelle
wasp la guêpe
watch *(noun)* la montre
  (verb) regarder
water l'eau
water heater le chauffe-eau
waterfall la chute d'eau
wave *(noun)* la vague
  (verb) faire signe de la main
wavy *(hair)* ondulé
we nous
weather le temps
website le site web
wedding le mariage
week la semaine
welcome: you're welcome
  je vous en prie
were: we were nous étions
  you were vous étiez
  they were ils/elles étaient
west l'ouest
wet mouillé

what? comment?
  what is it?
  qu'est-ce que c'est?
wheel la roue
wheelchair le fauteuil roulant
when? quand?
where? où?
whether si
which? lequel?
whiskey le whisky
white blanc, *(fem.)* blanche
who? qui?
why? pourquoi?
wide large
wife la femme
wind le vent
window la fenêtre
wine le vin
wine list la carte des vins
wine merchant le négociant en vins
wing l'aile
with avec
without sans
woman la femme
women *(restroom)* les toilettes pour
femmes
wood le bois
wool la laine
word le mot
work *(noun)* le travail
  (verb) travailler
  (machine etc.) fonctionner

worse pire
worst le pire
wrapping paper le papier d'emballage
  (for presents) le papier cadeau
wrench la clé anglaise
wrist le poignet
writing paper le papier à lettres
wrong faux, *(fem.)* fausse

year l'année
yellow jaune
yes oui
yesterday hier
yet déjà
  not yet pas encore
yogurt le yaourt
you vous
  (singular, familiar) tu
your: your house votre maison
  your shoes vos chaussures
  it's yours c'est à vous
  (singular, familiar)
  your book ton livre
  your house ta maison
  your shoes tes chaussures
  it's yours c'est à toi
youth hostel l'auberge de jeunesse

zipper la fermeture éclair®
zoo le zoo